# TROLLEYBUSES IN WEST CENTRAL LONDON

J2 997 is at the bottom of Pancras Road at Kings Cross working on route 613 to Holborn Circus on 8th May 1953; spick and span, it sports linen blinds in its route and destination blind boxes.

*London Transport Museum H16627*

# Published by Adam Gordon

It is Saturday 6th May 1961 – Cup Final day. K2 1205 is in Holborn and a few yards away from Holborn Circus terminus. Adjacent is the shop **A.W. GAMAGE LTD** (colloquially known as 'Gamages') where youngsters cajole parents to buy toys from this famous establishment. 1205 is a 543 so is working anti-clockwise around the Holborn loop.

*Peter Mitchell 1718*

**Front cover.** It is Tuesday 7th November 1961 and morning rain has delayed trolleybuses on routes involved in stage twelve of the trolleybus conversion scheme that takes place the next day. An inspector has told 1498 crew to curtail at **WINDSOR TERRACE CITY ROAD** rather than go through to Moorgate on the 609; there is not a bus stop here so passengers are being transferred there to M1 1547 which is going to Moorgate. There is no facing frog here so the conductor has moved the trolley arms onto the dead-end set of wires. He is about to replace the bamboo pole in its position beneath 1498 but its grappling hook trails along the roadway and under the front of 1547. Both vehicles have their interior and exterior lights switched on. The driver of 1498 has acted very professionally as he has stopped just beyond the power feeder and before the zebra crossing. Next day will see 1498 and 1547 at Fulwell depot – withdrawn.

*Tony Belton*

**Back cover.** Always at Edmonton depot, K2 1195 moves across the Regents canal bridge in Caledonian Road on 23rd December 1959. It is working to Holborn Circus on route 659 which it has been doing since February 1938.

*John Clark*

ISBN 978-1-910654-50-7

Publication no. 141

Published in 2023 by   Adam Gordon, Kintradwell Farmhouse, Brora, Sutherland, KW9 6LU
                       Tel: 01408 622660      E-mail: adam@ahg-books.com

Designed and typeset by   Barnabas Gordon
                          Tel: 07795 201 502      Email: Barney@ahgbooks.com

Printed by        Henry Ling Ltd., The Dorset Press, Dorchester, DT1 1HD

# INTRODUCTION

any trolleybus routes converged in the Central area; this led to a high number of vehicles and an abundance of overhead 'special ork'. Many of the junctions in this area had intricate layouts. The suburbs saw no more than four routes at their outer termini t in the Central area some had five or six. The following list (apart from the 565 which was withdrawn in October 1956) details e services that existed in the Central area when they were at their maximum - 6th January 1959. Photos credited to Denis ttams and Norman Rayfield are courtesy of the 2RT2 Preservation group. Those attributed to the London Transport Museum e credited to @TfL from the London Transport Museum Collection. Please note that there are a number of images that may pear cropped. However, these are as the photographer took them. As further interest, a number of war damage items have en included.

| | |
|---|---|
| 513 | Hampstead Heath to Holborn Circus – return to Parliament Hill Fields |
| 517 | North Finchley to Holborn Circus via Highgate |
| 521 | North Finchley to Holborn Circus via Wood Green |
| 543 | Wood Green to Holborn Circus |
| 565 | Barking to Holborn Circus |
| 609 | Barnet to Moorgate |
| 611 | Highgate Village to Moorgate |
| 613 | Parliament Hill Fields to Holborn Circus – return to Hampstead Heath |
| 615 | Parliament Hill Fields to Moorgate |
| 617 | North Finchley to Holborn Circus via Highgate |
| 621 | North Finchley to Holborn Circus via Wood Green |
| 627 | Waltham Cross to Tottenham Court Road |
| 629 | Enfield to Tottenham Court Road |
| 639 | Hampstead Heath to Moorgate |
| 641 | Winchmore Hill to Moorgate |
| 643 | Wood Green to Holborn Circus |
| 653 | Aldgate to Tottenham Court Road |
| 659 | Waltham Cross to Holborn Circus |
| 679 | Waltham Cross to Smithfield |
| 683 | Stamford Hill to Moorgate |

---

## 1910.—CONVERSION TO TROLLEYBUS OPERATION OF ROUTES Nos. 3, 5, 7 AND 15.

**Notice to Inspectors and Conductors.**

On Sunday, 10th July, 1938, Tram Routes Nos. 3, 5, 7 and 15 will be converted to trolleybus operation as shewn :—

| Tram Route No. | Trolleybus Route No. | Route. | Remarks. |
|---|---|---|---|
| 3 | 513 | Hampstead and Holborn/Farringdon Street Loop via Grays Inn Road | Hampstead Depot will be closed and trolleybuses will operate these services from Holloway Depot. |
| 7 | 613 | Parliament Hill Fields and Farringdon Street/Holborn Loop via Farringdon Road | |
| 5 | 639 | Hampstead and Moorgate (Finsbury Square)    ... ... | |
| 15 | 615 | Parliament Hill Fields and Moorgate (Finsbury Square) | |

**Route Numbers.**

Route No. 513 will be shewn on trolleybuses leaving Hampstead and will be retained until arriving back at Parliament Hill Fields. Route No. 613 will be shewn on trolleybuses leaving Parliament Hill Fields and will be retained until arriving back at Hampstead.

---

### AMENDMENTS TO TROLLEYBUSES IN EAST CENTRAL LONDON

| | |
|---|---|
| age 3 | Omitted on the routes list was route 677 which operated from Smithfield to West India Docks. It commenced on 10th September 1939 and finished on 14th April 1959. |
| age 70 | Trolleybus 1253 is a K2 class vehicle. |
| age 83 | Middle photo: 1458 is a West Ham depot vehicle while 1509 belongs to Poplar depot. |
| age 92 | Top photo: Trolleybus 1670 was an experimental trolleybus with AEC components. |
| age 103 | The bottom photo should be credited to Roy Hobbs not Ray Hobbs. |
| age 151 | Top photo: 1241 is in Essex Road, passing Englefield Road not Ockendon Road as stated. |
| age 161 | Top photo: The reference to 1348's blind should state that it shows part of the next display, not the previous one. |
| age 169 | The blind display is a facsimile of what was shown on Poplar's original destination blinds. |
| lap | This excluded the trolleybus routes that terminated at Aldgate – 567, 569, 653, 661 and 663. |

The overtaking wire [...] the south side at Moorga[...] greatly assisted the departu[...] of trolleybuses in more-or-le[...] the correct sequence; this [...] well illustrated by 1062 a[...] 1426 with the latter needi[...] to depart before the form[...] This view was taken on [...] Sunday when Highgate dep[...] had a five-vehicle allocati[...] on route 609. L3 1426 is on[...] going as far as North Finchl[...] on the 609; K1 1062 is goi[...] the full length of route 641 t[...] Winchmore Hill. *John Buck[...]*

Another way for on[...] trolleybus to get in front [...] another: involved are 1126 a[...] 1408 which are on the inn[...] set of wires. An inspecte[...] has signalled 1126's driver t[...] park in the position shown; h[...] and its conductor, each with [...] bamboo pole, are moving i[...] trolley booms from the insi[...] set of wires to the outside on[...] so that it can depart before L[...] 1408 which will soon leave f[...] Hampstead Heath on the 63[...] K1 1126 on the 641 is on[...] going as far as Turnpike Lan[...] Station. *Pamlin Prin[...]*

A further option for on[...] trolleybus to 'jump' anothe[...] was for the vehicle on th[...] inside track to have i[...] trolley arms placed under i[...] retaining hooks, thus allowi[...] another to pass. Illustratin[...] this, J1 945 on route 60[...] extends a courtesy to K[...] 1216 which is working on th[...] 683. Two bowstring arms ar[...] used for overhead support o[...] this side of Finsbury Squar[...]
*Michael Dryhur[...]*

Route 683 was the least frequent trolleybus service to be seen at Moorgate. The top two images show the display used by vehicles going to its northern terminus of Stamford Hill; 1098 sports 'linen' blinds while 1226 has a linen route blind and a 'paper' destination blind. Both vehicles are on the southern part of Finsbury Square; 1033 on the 611 is to the rear. In the lower view 1202, also at the loading point, shows the display for running into Stamford Hill depot. Until the 683's withdrawal after operations on 6th January 1959, eighty-nine trolleybuses an hour were scheduled to arrive and leave Moorgate in Monday to Friday peak hours.

*Alan Cross/
Anthony Wright/
Alan Cross*

An inspector has used his initiative and has found a way to ensure that all four trolleybuses in this view can leave in the correct order, initially that the last in line (1356) can get in front of the other three. 1328 has its trolley poles dropped, with 1352 and another vehicle behind on the inside track with their booms up. This allows 1356 on route 611 to pass all of them on the outside set of wires on 9th July 1960. Whether 1328 will third or fourth to leave is not known. *Ron Welling*

Route 611 was the last trolleybus route to be introduced to Moorgate - on 10th December 1939. There were two ways that the display for Highgate Village was shown on Charlton Works produced blinds; L1 1355 shows the original panel – J3 1038 shows the second one. The J3s and L1s had coasting and run back brakes fitted, a Ministry of Transport stipulation for trolleybus operation of Highgate Hill. The twenty-five J3s were deemed sufficient for the 611; however, in anticipation of it being projected to North Finchley fifteen L1s were delivered later. With the extension not taking place both classes were used on all routes working out of Holloway/Highgate depot.
*Alan Cross*

he 611 panel for Highgate Village on paper blinds manufactured at Aldenham Works is shown by L1 1360 on the stern side of Finsbury Square. This image was taken on a Sunday - the lack of other trolleybuses indicates this. bamboo pole hangs from a traction standard and an **ALIGHTING POINT ONLY** sign is attached to a traction le; the 'dolly' stop seems to have no use at the present time. *Tony Belton*

is 27th June 1939 and route 641 has been operating for just over a year. This view clearly shows a second wire the eastern side of Finsbury Square – whether it was fully frogged-in or was a dead-ender is unknown. H1 833 is its original deep rear wheel arches and silver roof; it is only going as far as Turnpike Lane. *Don Thompson*

On Sunday 16th July 1961 the Tramway Museum Society organised a trip over routes due for withdrawal two day later. Finchley's 1472 was used - participants await permission to board. L3 1472 has its poles on the wires; departure is not imminent, they will need to be dropped to allow other trolleybuses to pass. **FINSBURY SQUAR HOUSE** appears in many views taken at Moorgate.

*Don Lew*

In late 1959/early 1960 H1 815, on route 641 has just arrived at Moorgate; as the vehicle slows down, the drive winds the destination blind down a few inches - to show Winchmore Hill. The overtaking wire was removed man years ago.

HI 760 was allocated to Wood Green depot on 1st June 1938, staying in service there until 26th April 1960; standing at Moorgate on route 641 is therefore routine. 760's conductor has set its blinds perfectly for its next trip to Winchmore Hill on 16th September 1954. KI 1115 on route 683 has just arrived at Moorgate; it belongs to Stamford Hill depot so the Hackney Gazette advertisement is relevant to the routes it operates on. 1115 will pass to Wood Green depot in due course. Despite receiving a full overhaul in 1959 it was not deemed to be in a sufficiently good enough condition to join its sister vehicles (1113 - 1118) transferring to Isleworth in 1961.          *Ron Wellings*

| 683 | Stamford Hill (clockwise) |
| --- | --- |
| | †Stoke Newington, High Street (clockwise) |
| | Kingsland High Street, Crossway (clockwise) |
| | Kingsland Road, Downham Road (clockwise) 6.0 to 9.20 a.m.: 6.0 to 8.0 p.m. and * |
| | *New North Road/Baring Street (clockwise) |
| | Finsbury Square (clockwise) |

*Details of terminal and curtailment points for route 683. Two points:*
*-Route 683 does not pass Downham Road in Kingsland Road so is an erroneous entry.*
*-Mildmay Park is not given as a curtailment point despite route 683 passing through.*

| | | VEHICLE TIME CARD | | | | | | | | | | | |
|---|---|---|---|---|---|---|---|---|---|---|---|---|---|

**6971** VEHICLE TIME CARD   WINCHMORE HILL or TURNPIKE LANE STN. (UND.) and MOORGATE (Finsbury Square).   ROUTE 641
TIME SCHEDULE NUMBER   OPERATING ON **CHRISTMAS DAY**   LEAVE DEPOT. **9 45**   RUNNING NUMBER **W N 65**

| Winchmore Hill | Palmers Green | Wood Green | Redvers Road | Turnpike Lane Station | Manor House | Newington Green | Moorgate Arrive | Moorgate Leave | Newington Green | Manor House | Turnpike Lane Station | Redvers Road | Wood Green | Palmers Green | Winchmore Hill |
|---|---|---|---|---|---|---|---|---|---|---|---|---|---|---|---|
| | | 9 47 | | 9 57 | | 10.18 | 10.20 | | 10.41 | | | 10 51 | 11 5 | | |
| 11 8 | | 11 22 | | 11 32 | | 11 53 | 11 56 | | 12 17 | | | 12 27 | 12 41 | | |
| 12 44 | | 12 58 | | 1 8 | | 1 29 | 1 32 | | 1 53 | | | 2 3 | 2 17 | | |
| 2 20 | | 2 34 | | 2 44 | | 3 5 | 3 8 | | 3 29 | | | 3 39 | | | |
| | | | | | | | | | | | | DEPOT 3 41 | | | |

NOTE:— Both Driver and Conductor are responsible for the vehicle running to the times stated above.

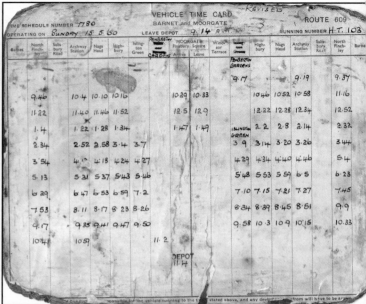

There was a tendency for trolleybuses moving from the north to the east side of Finsbury Square to 'lose' the positive trolley arm; 1443 on the 615 on 21st August 1960 and 1147 on route 641 another time are example Demolition is taking place in the lower view; are the workmen's huts linked to it? *Hugh Taylor/Peter Moor*

Buses on route 21 terminated at Moorgate; they were overtaken by trolleybuses daily with route 641 featuring in both these photographs. In the top view H1 847 passes RT 1273; in the lower image K2 1239 overtakes RT 2051 on the last day that trolleybuses will be seen here. The buses have lengthy trips ahead of them – to Sidcup garage in Kent.

*Lyndon Rowe/Peter Moore*

1054 was the highest numbered J3; it had a more rounded front dome than any other member of the class and to trolleybus connoisseurs, had a different appearance. Approaching Moorgate, 1054 is in City Road on 17th July 1960; the driver has prematurely changed the destination blind for its next trip to Highgate Village on route 611. On the left is the entrance to Finsbury Barracks.

*Peter Mitchell 15501*

L1 1367 has left Moorgate and is just a few yards away from Old Street station; the fact that it shows **HIGHGATE ARCHWAY STATION** means it is running into Highgate depot – all 611s from the south had to use the MacDonal Road/Salisbury Road loop by Archway before running-in. At the same location 1361 is going the full length of rout 611 to Highgate Village with 844 behind heading to Winchmore Hill on the 641; this view was taken in the first ha of the 1950s as both vehicles have linen blinds fitted. The clock attached to 21 City Road (Printers and Stationer shows that these images were taken just six minutes apart, but on different days (1.35pm/1.41pm).

*Roy Hubble/Martin Brow*

n the aforementioned TMS tour 1472 had to use battery mode to move from Old Street into City Road. Using
bamboo pole the Finchley conductor has placed the positive arm on City Road wiring; the negative boom will
llow.
*J.H. Price*

l 1358 passes through the Old Street/City Road junction while working to Highgate Village on route 611 on a wet
aturday - 9th July 1960; L1 1355 is in front with another 615 going the other way. Plenty of traffic for trolleybuses
contend with. The traffic signal on the left stating 'GO' is illuminated; a bamboo pole is hooked onto a traction
andard on the right. An all-action photograph enhanced by rain.
*Jack Gready*

HR2 tram 153 is in City Roa[d]
approaching Old Street statio[n];
it is a conduit-only car. The H[R]
designation meant 'hilly rout[e];
route 11 required cars of th[is]
class to be used on Highga[te]
Hill. A 641 is about to enter Ea[st]
Road.                    *H.B. Priest[ley]*

K2 1334 has just passed throug[h]
the City Road/East Road facin[g]
frog while operating northboun[d]
on route 641.  Note the facin[g]
frog apparatus; a semi-automat[ic]
frog handle and re-set ska[te]
- only 609s use it now. Th[e]
photographer was meticulo[us]
with the descriptions he wrote [on]
the back of his pictures; this o[ne]
states: HOXTON   CITY ROA[D]
LKG NORTH    EAST ROA[D]
FORKING RIGHT  5 OCT 6[ ]
                    *John Gillha[m]*

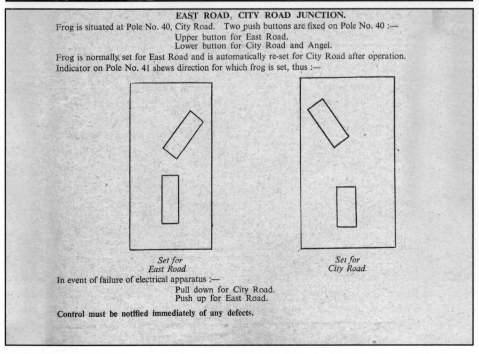

**EAST ROAD, CITY ROAD JUNCTION.**

Frog is situated at Pole No. 40, City Road.   Two push buttons are fixed on Pole No. 40 :—
Upper button for East Road.
Lower button for City Road and Angel.

Frog is normally set for East Road and is automatically re-set for City Road after operation.
Indicator on Pole No. 41 shews direction for which frog is set, thus :—

*Set for East Road.*                          *Set for City Road.*

In event of failure of electrical apparatus :—
Pull down for City Road.
Push up for East Road.

**Control must be notified immediately of any defects.**

K1 1269 powers through the East Road/City Road junction on 7th November 1961. It follows a motorbus on trolleybus replacement route 271 – maybe a bit too close! 1269 was a late addition to Wood Green's fleet, being sent there on 1st June 1961; therefore, it only worked on route 641 while allocated to WN.
*Peter Paye*

Routes 611 and 641 were the last routes that used East Road. This view was taken one Sunday with K2 1200 on the 641, with 1033 on route 611 behind, approaching City Road junction. *Don Thompson*

There is a sparsity of pedestrians and traffic in this view that was taken on the last Sunday of operation – 17th July 1960. J3 1048 is at the bottom of East Road where it joins City Road while working on route 611 to Moorgate; note the shadow of the trailing frog on the roadway. Dawson's was a local department store, with this location known colloqially as 'Dawson's Corner'.
*Tony Belton*

J3 1044 is by Haberdasher Street in East Road heading for Moorgate on the last Sunday of operation of route 6[?] – 17th July 1960. After 1044 has been put to bed that night it will have just two more days in service, as it will b[?] withdrawn the following Tuesday. *Peter Mitchell 1549*

J3 1049 is by Bookham Street in New North Road on 1st November 1958 so route 611 is in no immediate threat [of] withdrawal. The photographer is obtaining his London trolleybus images well before conversion to buses reache[d] this point. Messrs Clarke and Mitchell who were good friends have given different descriptions of this location i[n] their indexes for the views on pages 16 and 17. *John Clark[e]*

Whilst filming route 611 in its death throes the photographer took the opportunity to capture some 641s which was the other route that traversed East Road/New North Road at the time. 1199 is by Murray Grove (on the left) and where New North Road runs into East Road - 1274 is by Grange Street, a short way north; it is 17th July 1960 and both have nine months' service ahead of them at Wood Green depot. At stage ten of the trolleybus conversion scheme, they will move to Isleworth depot where their fortunes will be very varied; Isleworth were receiving K1s to replace Q1s. 1199, a K2, was sent in error – it languished in IH for six months before going for scrap. K1 1274 was put into service immediately; just over a year later it became the last 657 and therefore the last trolleybus to enter Isleworth depot which it did just a few minutes into 9th May 1962. In doing so it became the last Leyland trolleybus to operate on the streets of Great Britain.

*Peter Mitchell 15497/15496*

7th November 1961, not only the last day of rou[te]
641 but also the last day that KI 1154 works f[or]
London Transport. It is just north of Murray Gro[ve]
in New North Road; 1154 is a few minutes into [its]
journey to Winchmore Hill.          *Peter Pa[?]*

Monday 20th March, 1950

    2.05 p.m. East Road, Hoxton.  Linesman working in vicinity
when current failed from Poles 2 - 24.
                             4 mins. Passenger delay.
    2.30 p.m. Poles 2 - 32 linked by Linesman when arc
across switches occurred in feeder pillar: East Road, Hoxton.
                          12 mins. Passenger delay.

KI 1061 is only going to Newington Green on th[e]
641; it is in New North Road and slightly furth[er]
north than the previous photograph.   Som[e]
morning and evening Monday to Friday peak ho[ur]
trips only went as far as this shortworking point[;]
this increased seating capacity on the southern e[nd]
of the route.          *Peter Moo[re?]*

ew North Road had a wide thoroughfare and at Dorchester Street its width seems too generous for the little
affic using it. J3 1042 has been operating on the 611 for many a year and during its lifetime has worked to
oorgate thousands of times. It is 5th May 1956.

*Peter Mitchell 8597*

the summer of 1960, L1 1366 has just passed through the **New North Road/Baring Street** facing frog which
ables routes 611 and 641 to go their separate ways. Small boys position themselves beside 1366 which heads
r the 611's northern terminus of **Highgate Village**.

*Tony Belton*

L1 1367 is only going as far as **NAGS HEAD HOLLOWAY**. It has been running late so an inspector has told th[e] crew to run it into **Highgate depot** - maybe the crew will allow passengers to travel as far as **Pemberton Garde[ns]** from where 1367 will access the depot. Going the other way at Baring Street junction is L1 1359. *Tony Belt*

Route 611 has been withdrawn as evidenced by just a single set of wires over the Regents Canal bridge in N[...] North Road; K1 1263 had previously been at Clapton depot but now resides at Wood Green. Another 641 [is?] going to Newington Green. *Fred*

A number of the frogs and crossovers at the Baring Street/New North Road junction are seen on 1st November 1958. Moving from Baring Street into New North Road on route 641 is one of Wood Green's stalwarts – H1 756 which advertises Bertram Mills Circus at Olympia. *John Clarke*

These two images show the change of class of trolleybus that occurred at Wood Green depot mainly between 1959 and 1960 - H1s being replaced by K1s/K2s. It is 9th July 1960 and a 'Buses for Trolleybuses' poster announcing the withdrawal of route 611 ten days later has been pasted onto a traction standard on the left. Heading south are J3 1053 on the 611 and K1 1147 on the 641; heading north on the 611 is L1 1361. *Jack Gready*

It is 7th May 1961 and route 611 has long gone; London Transport's overhead staff have removed all 'special work' at the Baring Street/New North Road junction. They have made an excellent symmetrical job of the revised wiring; 641's trolley arms will follow the overhead perfectly. K1 1284 heads for Moorgate; on the right and over the other side of the wall is Regents Canal. *Peter Mitchell 17227*

K1 1116 on route 641 is at the bottom of Baring Street on 19th July 1960 and about to turn left into New Nort
Road; it uses the regular track having just passed the facing frog that takes shortworking 611s back toward
Highgate. There are two sets of wires going the other way: the right-hand one is for Southgate Road with the le
one being a shortworking facility - mainly for curtailed southbound 611s.                                    *Alan Cro*

The Baring Street shortworking was extensively used by 641s; K2 1239 waits out time. For many years a Clapto
depot vehicle, it spent two and a half years at Wood Green; par for the course, their maintenance staff have turne
it out in excellent condition.                                                                          *Peter Moor*

aring Street loop was also used by curtailed 611s and on Bank Holiday Mondays when an enhanced service perated between here and Highgate Village when twenty vehicles were allocated to the route – far higher than ne Monday to Friday total. The facing frog in the loop was set for 641s heading north; therefore, 1355's conductress ulls the frog handle down so that it can regain New North Road on 6th May 1959. Baring Street was also a turning oint for buses on route 76; RTW 104 has its blind set for its home base - TOTTENHAM GARAGE.       *John Clarke*

oute 641 used the Baring Street turn-back far more frequently than the other two services (611 and 683) that sed this facility. Illustrating the 641 on 14th October 1961 K1 1277 is about to leave the right-hand side of the iangle of streets that all came under the name of Baring Street. In view is one of the trailing frogs, a facing frog nd the crossover at the exit. The styling of the houses in Baring Street were unique to the Hoxton area.

*Jack Gready*

Route 683 was never a mone
spinner and over the years i
frequency was reduced un
withdrawn after operatir
on 6th January 1959; abo
to pass through one of th
two trailing frogs from Barir
Street loop K1 1136 hea
for Moorgate. Of interest w
a single Monday to Frid
evening trip that turned he
before returning to Moorgat
this was for scheduling reaso
rather than an operatir
purpose.    *Peter Mitchell 1144*

Exemplifying the '6 I
shortworking curve' L1 135
turns right from Baring Stre
into New North Road; th
driver will need to change th
destination blind for his nex
northbound trip. Intriguing
there are a few passenge
on board – they know th
given the opportunity the
can board in Baring Stre
and head north on a 611 fror
within the curtailment are
*Fred Iv*

L1 1359's positive trolley arr
has drifted off the overhea
when passing through th
Baring Street trailing frc
a bit too quickly. The driv
is rectifying the situation s
that he can get on his way t
Highgate Village on route 61
*Tony Belto*

| T/C No. | Drawing No. | Location | Date of Approval | Route and direction of Turn | Remarks |
|---------|-------------|----------|------------------|------------------------------|---------|
| 131 | F.2947 | New North Road, Baring St. | 1. 9.38 | Clockwise via the two legs of Baring St. and then New Baring St. | Limited to emergency only. |

611s accessing Baring Street shortworking needed their trolley arms to be swung from the main line onto a dead-end set of wires in New North Road; 1358 illustrates this. When operating Highgate Village to Baring Street 'shorts' on Bank holidays, six frog pulls and a trolley swing were required. 1358 advertises booze – VAT 69 Scotch Whisky and Ben Truman Ale.

*Tony Belton*

J3 1052 is by Wilton Villas in New North Road while working yet another mundane trip to Moorgate; in the background is the North Pole public house. Route 611 was worked on a separate rota at Highgate depot with regular crews; bearing in mind the short length of the route it must have been very monotonous. It is 15th July 1960, the last Friday of operation of route 611.

*Peter Mitchell 15460*

As Essex Road was approached there was an incline that trolleybuses had to climb; this is illustrated by L1 1359 which is about to move through the Essex Road/New North Road junction on the last day of route 611 – 19th July 1960. The traffic signal in view is cantilevered from a pole on the pavement. *Alan Cross*

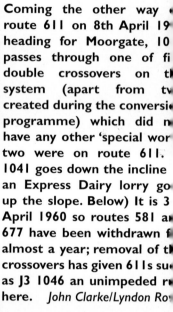

Coming the other way
route 611 on 8th April 19
heading for Moorgate, 10
passes through one of fi
double crossovers on t
system (apart from t
created during the conversi
programme) which did n
have any other 'special wor
two were on route 611.
1041 goes down the incline
an Express Dairy lorry go
up the slope. Below) It is 3
April 1960 so routes 581 a
677 have been withdrawn f
almost a year; removal of t
crossovers has given 611s su
as J3 1046 an unimpeded r
here.  *John Clarke/Lyndon Ro*

Canonbury Road was not or
of the most salubrious stree
in north London; this ima
is indexed as being taken
New River Walk which impli
an up-market location. 10
heads for Moorgate on t
611 on 5th May 1956.
*Peter Mitchell 85*

LI 1360 is in Canonbury Road by Canonbury Square; running late it is only going to BARING STREET NEW NORTH RD. It will be observed that in photographs featuring route 611 in its later days, many vehicles still used linen route blinds; these had been manufactured about ten years previously – very sturdy material bearing in mind the extensive use made of them at Highgate depot. *Tony Belton*

By Compton Avenue in Canonbury Road on 5th May 1956, LI 1355 on route 611 heads for Moorgate. Highgate depot were not known for turning vehicles out in good external condition; in this instance they have 'bucked the trend'.

*Peter Mitchell 8595*

J3 1051 is at the top end of Canonbury Road and heads for Moorgate; route 611 was never operated by any other depot than Holloway/Highgate. In the far background a trolleybus is seen at Highbury Corner. *Tony Belton*

In Canonbury Road and just before Highbury Corner on 31st March 1958 are examples of both classes of trolleybuses that were permitted to operate on Highgate Hill which was the preserve of route 611. 1039 heads towards Moorgate while L1 1359 makes its way to Highgate Village.

*John Clark*

These views, taken on 31st March 1958, illustrate Highbury Corner before major alterations were made to roadways and trolleybus overhead layouts there. 1040 heads for Highgate Village on the 611 as L1 135 makes its way to Moorgate on the same route. Even in the late 1950s, cobbles could still be seen on some of London's main thoroughfares; traffic of various sizes is seen in both views. The photographer is standing in the part of St Paul's Road which is about to 'disappear'.

*John Clark*

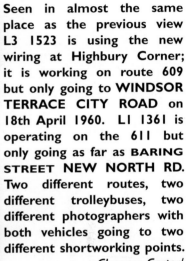

Seen in almost the same place as the previous view L3 1523 is using the new wiring at Highbury Corner; it is working on route 609 but only going to **WINDSOR TERRACE CITY ROAD** on 18th April 1960. L1 1361 is operating on the 611 but only going as far as **BARING STREET NEW NORTH RD.** Two different routes, two different trolleybuses, two different photographers with both vehicles going to two different shortworking points.

*Clarence Carter/*
*Don Thompson*

John Sugrue and Sons Ltd are the company tasked by the London County Council to install the new roundabout and roadway revisions at Highbury Corner (in place of a two-way junction). Although there is still a lot of work to do, a roadway has been laid so that vehicles can move from Holloway Road, around a partly constructed roundabout and into Upper Street. Illustrating this is Edmonton's 1184 which is working on route 679 to Smithfield.

*Fred Ivey*

E3 car 1932, working on route 35 to Highgate, is at the very end of Upper Street and moving into Holloway Road by Highbury and Islington station on 15th March 1952.

Ostensibly in Upper Street, K2 1171 on route 679 moves past roadworks on 31st March 1958 - a 609 follows; in the background is a southbound 611. Oil drums and planks of wood indicate to pedestrians that this is a no-go area; re-positioned traction poles, initial span wire work and a new trailing frog are in view. Not yet erected is the crossover which will be installed at the point where 1171's trolley arms are seen.
*John Clarke*

M1 1544 on route 609 has dewired; both trolley arms left the wires as it circled Highbury Corner. The booms have crossed themselves which means that the crew will have to spend a couple of minutes sorting the situation out.
*Tony Belton*

J3 1053, a 611 to Highgate Village, is using the new roundabout at Highbury Corner on 14th July 1960. The revised overhead changes came into effect in October 1958. Eleven houses were demolished in the process; the cost of the overhead alterations would have been met by the local traffic authority.
*Peter Mitchell 15456*

23rd April 1961 with the photographer having a day with trolleybus routes that are to be withdrawn in two days' time – at stage ten of the conversion programme. Working on the 679 to Smithfield, K3 1687 is having its pole returned to the overhead following a dewirement at Highbury Corner. Bit of a dewirement spot here the...
*Peter Mitchell 171*

Entering Upper Street at Highbury Corner on 5th March 1961 is N1 1574; this is a Sunday when Highgate had small 609 allocation. It had moved in from Bow depot following the withdrawal of route 695 on 6th January 195... That month, many less recently overhauled vehicles of a number of classes were moved from depots affected service cuts at that time to depots where they would be withdrawn before more recently overhauled specimen of the same class. This meant that 1574 was withdrawn at Highgate depot at stage ten of the conversion schem whereas the majority of N1s survived until stage thirteen.
*Peter Mitchell 168-*

Trolleybus 924 on route 609 and motorbus RTL 1624 on bus route 30 are adjacent to each other in Upper Street; 924 has been working along this thoroughfare for many years. Not so RTL 1624 which was one of many RTLs that were stored as surplus to requirements when delivered in 1954 and that rested without tyres on wooden blocks in various garages for up to four years. Now that some older RTLs have been sold, these 'new' ones are being released into service – without adverts. RTL 1624's destination blind looks new; the other blinds have been used before. Bearing in mind that RTL 1624 was first licensed on 1st March 1958 and that this view was taken on 1st March 1958 this is a case of saying 'Well done young man' to:

*John Clarke*

**VEHICLE TIME CARD**  REVISED  **ROUTE 609**
BARNET and MOORGATE

TIME SCHEDULE NUMBER 7780  3  RUNNING NUMBER H.T. 103
OPERATING ON *Sunday 15.5.60*  LEAVE DEPOT 9.14 A.M.

| Barnet | North Finchley | Salisbury Road | Archway Station | Nags Head | High-bury | Islington Green | PEMBERTON GARDENS / MOORGATE Finsbury Square Arrive | Leave | Windsor Terrace | Green / PEMBERTON GARDENS | High-bury | Nags Head | Archway Station | Salisbury Road | North Finchley | Barnet |
|---|---|---|---|---|---|---|---|---|---|---|---|---|---|---|---|---|
| | | | | | | | | | | 9.17 | | | 9.19 | | 9.37 | |
| | 9.46 | 10.4 | 10.10 | 10.16 | | 10.29 | | 10.33 | | | 10.46 | 10.52 | 10.58 | | 11.16 | |
| | 11.22 | 11.40 | 11.46 | 11.52 | | 12.5 | | 12.9 | | | 12.22 | 12.28 | 12.34 | | 12.52 | |
| | 1.4 | 1.22 | 1.28 | 1.34 | | 1.47 | | 1.49 | | ISLINGTON GREEN | 2.2 | 2.8 | 2.14 | | 2.32 | |
| | 2.34 | 2.52 | 2.58 | 3.4 | 3.7 | | | | | 3.9 | 3.14 | 3.20 | 3.26 | | 3.44 | |
| | 3.54 | 4.12 | 4.18 | 4.24 | 4.27 | | | | | 4.29 | 4.34 | 4.40 | 4.46 | | 5.4 | |
| | 5.13 | 5.31 | 5.37 | 5.43 | 5.46 | | | | | 5.48 | 5.53 | 5.59 | 6.5 | | 6.23 | |
| | 6.29 | 6.47 | 6.53 | 6.59 | 7.2 | | | | | 7.10 | 7.15 | 7.21 | 7.27 | | 7.45 | |
| | 7.53 | 8.11 | 8.17 | 8.23 | 8.26 | | | | | 8.34 | 8.39 | 8.45 | 8.51 | | 9.9 | |
| | 9.17 | 9.35 | 9.41 | 9.47 | 9.50 | | | | | 9.58 | 10.3 | 10.9 | 10.15 | | 10.33 | |
| | 10.41 | 10.59 | | | | 11.2 | | | | | | | | | | |
| | | | | | | DEPOT 11.4 | | | | | | | | | | |

Conductor responsible for the vehicle running to the time stated above, and any deviation from will have to be ar...

ROAD POWER SERVICES – TROLLEYBUSES (CONTD.)

Friday, 10th November, 1950

7.30 p.m. Highbury Corner. Broken trolley wire.
6 mins. Passenger Delay.

E3 tramcar 186 on route [35] is passing Canonbury Lane [in] Upper Street on Saturday 15th March 1952; it heads sou[th] to Forest Hill. Those wishi[ng] to travel between Highbu[ry] Corner and Islington canno[t] only use the tram but als[o] motorbuses on routes 4, 19, 3[0,] 43 and trolleybuses on rout[es] 609 and 679.

*Peter Mitchell 32[...]*

It is often quoted that the L2s comprised nine vehicles (1370 – 1378); this is not the case as there were ten wi[th] 954, an experimental vehicle, being incorporated into the class. Allocated to Holloway depot in 1939 it stayed the[re] until February 1957 when a transfer to Finchley occurred. The driver doesn't know it, the photographer won't ha[ve] known it but this is 954's last day in service, and a wet one at that - it is Tuesday 25th April 1961, conversion sta[ge] ten. Between stages nine and ten of the programme L2 954 was the lowest numbered trolleybus in the fleet a[nd] the only one remaining vehicle with an ELB registration. Working on route 609 to Barnet, 954 heads down t[he] slope from Upper Street on the approach to Highbury Corner - at virtually the same location as the view abov[e.]

*Dave Pears[e]*

1521 is at Cross Street in Upper Street on 5th March 1961 with blinds perfectly set for its trip to Moorgate the 609. As all London trolleybus 'gricers' know, 1521 became the last trolleybus to operate on the streets of London; it entered Fulwell depot at about 1.10am on Wednesday 9th May 1962. *Peter Mitchell 16839*

am 173 on route 35 has just rounded a slight curve in Upper Street and heads towards Highbury Corner. action pole 123 indicates the location of this view which was taken outside the Mitre pub which purveys arrington's Ale and Stout. The local authority has kept the roadway in excellent condition; London Transport ck maintenance staff are their equals in presentation. *Don Thompson*

E3 tram 1921 failed somewhere north of the Kingsway subway on 15th March 1952; breakdown wagon 17!
(attached to the erstwhile Camberwell depot) pushed it to Providence Place by Islington Green where its damag
plough was removed along with its broken plough carrier. It was working on route 35 to Highgate; SPECIA
has been wound up on its rear blind – a strange description for a breakdown! A few minutes later assistance
being given by E3 1908 which is by St Mary's Path in Upper Street; it pushes 1921 northwards. Once the two ca
approached Pemberton Gardens they were uncoupled, with 1921 using the trolleybus overhead until it got
Pemberton Gardens, with an inspector accompanying it on foot. The inspector was breaking a rule in that tran
were not supposed to use trolleybus overhead under any circumstances! 1921 continued to use the trolleyb
overhead to reach Highgate depot where it was repaired. 175K is positioned in the nearside roadway in the low
view. What a performance!

*Peter Mitchell 3213/32*

lington Green loop was regularly used by scheduled and shortworking trolleybuses; the entrance to the loop
om both directions is seen in these views. In the top one K2 1233 heads to Smithfield on the 679; in the lower
nage L3 1505 is travelling to Moorgate on route 609.
*Don Thompson*

Much of the 609 Sunday afternoon and evening service only went as far as Islington Green where 1480 is parked on the cobbles at 3.26pm on 19th March 1961; it is a dull afternoon so the driver has switched the interior and exterior lights on. In the background are shops typical of the era - notably Collins Electrical Ltd and DAVE WAX who as North London's top tailor 'WELCOMES YOU'.

*Peter Mitchell 169*

| 609 | Barnet Church (clockwise) |
|---|---|
| | *New Barnet, Station Road (clockwise) battery |
| | North Finchley, 'Tally Ho' (clockwise) |
| | East Finchley Station (clockwise) |
| | Highgate, Archway Station (clockwise) |
| | Holloway, Warlters Road (clockwise) before 7.30 a.m.: after 7.0 p.m. and * |
| | Islington Green (clockwise and anti-clockwise) |
| | City Road |
| | *(1) Macclesfield Road (clockwise) battery |
| | (2) Windsor Terrace (clockwise) Bank holidays Summer Sundays and * |
| | Finsbury Square (clockwise) |

**2102.—ROUTE No. 609 EX TO OPERATE ON DECEMBER 26th & 27th.**

Notice to Inspectors and Conductors—Finchley Depot.

On December 26th and 27th, Route No. 609 EX Tally Ho Corner and Islington Green will operate from Finchley Depot. Route No. 517/617 tickets will be used which provide for journeys on Route No. 609.

Destination blinds must be set as follows :—

When running to Tally Ho Corner shew :—

No. 13 { Via Highgate / NORTH / FINCHLEY

When running to Islington Green shew :—

No. 28 { ISLINGTON / GREEN

A farebill for Route No. 609 will be exhibited in the depot.

L3 1452 is the subject of a time exposure; it is parked outside Collins Music Hall on the Islington Green shortworking wires. The destination blind has been turned for its trip to Barnet on the 609. *Brian Pa...*

Although 679s were frequently curtailed at Islington Green, photographs of them in the loop are rare; however, on Bank Holiday Monday 3rd April 1961 P1 1705 was caught on camera there. Note that the front destination blind is a 'paper' one while the rear one is of linen manufacture; it should also be observed that the Aldenham style route blinds are in different styles.

*Hugh Taylor*

On 9th October 1961, the penultimate Sunday of route 609; L3 1528 is working an 'Islington Green short'. It was one of six L3s (the others being 1470-1472 and 1527 and 1529) fitted with sliding window openers rather than half-drops; apart from 1470 these non-standard items were retained throughout their lives. 1528 moves from Essex Road, back into Upper Street; the driver has yet to change the destination blind. The overhead junction in the background was until stage two of the conversion programme used principally by 581s/677s heading for Bloomsbury and Smithfield respectively. With their withdrawal in April 1959 the frog setting was altered so that priority was given to shortworking 609s/679s heading back towards Holloway – the only use for the wiring between here and the overhead junction on the approach to Angel Islington would be for any 609 Moorgate to Archway Station shortworking curtailed at Islington Green.

*Peter Mitchell 19469*

Following the conversion of tram route 11 to trolleybus route 611 on 10th December 1939, three tram routes still operated in north London; 31, 33 and 35. In the top view E/1 180 is parked on the inner of the three tracks at Islington Green – it will soon be off to Wandsworth on the 31. In the second image - on 5th April 1952 - car number one having been selected by the LRTA, is having a day out on the 'north side' – a rare treat from its usual south London area; behind, a 609 makes its way to Moorgate. In the third view HR2 1862 is on a tour and shows SPECIAL, E3 197 heads for New Cross on route 35 while trolley-less HR2 104 works to HIGHGATE on route 35. This location was displayed on blinds as either AGRICULTURAL HALL or ISLINGTON GREEN. An inspector monitors the situation. Note the trolleybus trailing frog from Essex Road and the three-tier pavement in Upper Street.

*Top photo Don Thompson*

am tracks in Upper Street were lifted many years ago; 928 working on the 609 to Moorgate on 8th April 1959 sn't had to bump over the cobbles here for seven years. It has just passed through the crossover that brings ington Green shortworking vehicles back into Upper Street. The Royal Mail van is about twenty years younger an the trolleybus.

*John Clarke*

lington sub-station was at the south-east end of Islington High Street. Regularly and strategically parked there as a tower wagon which could be called into action at a moment's notice. Exemplifying this is **AEC Mercury** agon 85Q which is attached to **ELECTRICAL EQUIPMENT ENGINEER HOLLOWAY.** The view was taken on h October 1953; bearing in mind that Holloway depot had been re-named Highgate depot on 12th July 1950 the vised name needs to be put in place – and soon!

*John Gillham*

This view shows the facing frog in Islington High Street where 609s/679s went their different ways. This view was taken on 30th April 1961; route 679 has been defunct for four days; despite this 609 conductors still pull the frog handle for Moorgate – the erstwhile 679 still has priority! London Transport overhead staff will soon remove this piece of equipment and 609s will have a 'free run' here. Note the three tier pavement on the left. *John Gillham*

Islington Upper Street, one of Finchley's original vehicles, J1 925, heads for Barnet on the 609. As can be seen, Islington is very busy in this late 1950's view. *Michael Dryhurst*

L3 1472 heads south towards Moorgate on the 609; following it is a 'top-box' RT on route 19. L3 1472 is on the long lead-in between the facing frog and Islington Angel - nine traction poles in length, the longest on the system and maybe even in Britain. 1472 is in Islington High Street. *Anthony Wright*

h March 1961 and L3 1519 on the 609 moves from Islington High Street into City Road. Routes 615/639 were moved from the schedules after 31st January 1961; London Transport linesmen were tasked with removing all dundant 'special work' at this location as soon as possible after that date. They have almost finished the job with st the Pentonville Road/St John Street crossover to go; note the splices in the overhead where a crossover has en removed.

*Peter Mitchell 16838*

inesmen had returned to Islington Angel by 12th March 1961 (the date of this view) and removed the crossover entioned in the view above; K2 1346 passes through on its way to Smithfield on route 679. Soon after its ithdrawal on the night of 25th/26th April 1961 linesmen will return to this location and remove the wiring to nd from St John Street. This will just leave plain wiring from City Road into Islington High Street for route 609.

*Denis Battams*

Due to a shortage of trams, four trolley-less HR2s that had been withdrawn at stage six of the tram conversion programme in January 1952 were reinstated to New Cross shortly afterwards. It is Saturday 5th April 1952, the last day of trams in North London – it is unlikely that many people in this view would be aware of it. HR2 121, on route 35 to Forest Hill, is at the traffic lights at Angel Islington; C3 302 on route 609 heads for Barnet. An RTL can be seen behind the lorry, meaning that all three forms of London Transport's road passenger vehicles are in view. The four HR2 trams referred to above were the last trams that purely operated in conduit mode; route 35 was the last all-conduit service so there was no more use for them after this date.

*Julian Thompson courtesy Online Transport Archive*

Routes 609 and 679 travelled together between Nags Head Holloway and Islington Angel where they diverged. K2 1230 932 turns left into City Road on the 609 while K2 1230 will head down St John Street on route 679. *Don Thompson*

1424 was allocated to Holloway depot from new. Working on route 609 it has just turned from Islington High Street into City Road; behind is RT 2030 on route 133. L3 1424 is about to pass through the trailing frog at the top of City Road. *Fred Ivey*

M1 1546, a 615 to Moorgate, passes through the trailing frog at the corner of Islington High Street and City Road. 1546 had previously been at West Ham depot before arriving at Highgate in April 1960; in April 1961 it will be forwarded to Finchley depot where it would stay until withdrawn in November 1961. *Tony Belton*

1411 was one of twenty-three L3s sent to Holloway depot in 1939. It is at 'Angel Islington' on the 615 on 1st November 1958 having moved from Pentonville Road into City Road; it has just passed the frog that takes 677s down Goswell Road. *John Clarke*

To give greater seating capacity
the Woolwich area for war wor
Holloway depot exchanged its H
with most of Bexleyheath's B2s
the summer of 1939; Holloway
118 is an example of this. In 19.
Highgate's B2s were replaced I
C1s that had been replaced I
Q1s at Fulwell and Isleworth. 16
arrived from FW and is seen c
18th April 1953; both vehicles a
639s. The single entrance to Ang
underground station is in th
background of both images.

*Lower photo Clarence Cart*

On 6th September 1961, L3 1468 on route 609 is taking on a good load of passengers at the first stop in City Roa
It is positioned beyond the electrical power feeder – this means that drivers have an unimpeded getaway from thi
stop.

*Clarence Carte*

Further down City Road and outside the City Arms public house are two trolleybuses that regularly passed this establishment. 544 is one of three D3s allocated to Highgate depot for many years. J1 925 is a Finchley stalwart; their maintenance staff have embellished the ends of its trolley arms with white paint. 544 on the 639 and 925 on route 609 both head for Moorgate.

*Roy Vincent*

The 609 service is not doing very well as three are running together one hot afternoon; first in line is L3 1509 which is having its trolley arms moved from the main line wiring to the dead-end set of wires. When the weather was hot, traction wires tended to expand and would explain the looseness of the negative wire on which 1509's

Windsor Terrace 'dead-ender' in City Road looking south on 7th November 1961, the last day of route 609. L3 1487 heads for Barnet on its final day in service; in the evening it will be driven to Stonebridge depot where, after a few days, in their dumping area will make one last trip under power – to a scrapyard behind Colindale depot.    *Peter Paye*

| 639 | Hampstead, South End Green (clockwise) |
| --- | --- |
| | *Prince of Wales Road 'Mother Shipton' (clockwise) battery |
| | Mornington Crescent (clockwise) |
| | City Road |
| | *(1)  Macclesfield Road (clockwise) battery |
| | (2)  Windsor Terrace (clockwise, Bank holidays: summer Sundays and * |
| | Finsbury Square (clockwise) |

This item shows two curtailment points within 50 yards: Macclesfield Road and Windsor Terrace.

The regularity of the service is so bad another time that two consecutive 609s have been curtailed at Windsor Terrace – dusk approaches so both have all their lights switched on. L3 1519 is the first of the pair; L3 1474 behind has its destination blind already changed to show BARNET. Both vehicles have to use the 'dead end' wires here.    *Tony Belton*

In November 1952 Highgate depot was given some Sunday and Bank Holiday work on route 609; with just five vehicles allocated it was rare to see their 1424 using Windsor Terrace loop. The driver has turned here on many occasions as he knows how far he can go into Windsor Terrace without dewiring; his conductor moves the trolley arms onto the loop wire. To the left is pole A59; the loop had seven poles in the 59 sequence - they ran from A59 to G59 with G59 being the highest suffixed pole on the system. Another trolleybus is parked further round the loop.    *Peter Moore*

Inconsiderate parking cause[d] problems for trolleybuses turni[ng] in Windsor Terrace as shown by th[is] view of 1509 on the 609. The re[ar] offside wheels are on the paveme[nt] and it looks as if the driver w[ill] just be able to squeeze past th[e] bollards that have been positione[d] to prevent indiscriminate parkin[g]. No doubt 1509s front offside whe[el] had to mount the kerb too.

*Fred Iv[ey]*

Highgate's 1370 was the first L2 [of] the main batch and is working [on] route 639 when photographed [at] **WINDSOR TERRACE CITY ROA[D]** loop on 23rd July 1960. In the t[op] view it is parked under a bracke[t] arm; in the lower image it leave[s] for Hampstead Heath. Withdraw[n] at stage nine of the conversio[n] programme (1st February 196[1]) it was reinstated to Stonebrid[ge] depot exactly one month late[r] (1st March 1961). Unfortunate[ly] it suffered a burnt-out tractio[n] motor near the end of Augu[st] and was immediately withdraw[n].

*Peter Mitchell 15571/1557[2]*

| 639 | Hampstead | & Moorgate | 2/7½ | 15 | 15 | 15 | 7163 | 529 | Highgate | 29 | 29 | – | See Rte. 513 |
| 639 | Hampstead | & Windsor Terrace | –/7½ | 15 | 15 | 15 | | | | | | | |
| 639 | Hampstead | & Kings Cross | – | – | 10½ | 10½ | 7170 | 527 | Highgate | 7 | 7 | 9 | Supp. Schedule |

| 639 | Moorgate & Hampstead | ... | M-F. | 8 | 5½ | 9 | 5½ | 7261 | 439 | Highgate | 8 | TB | 8 | 1 add. ex R. 615 |
| 639 | Moorgate & Hampstead | ... | Sat. | 6 | 7½ | 7½ | 9/6½ | 7264 | 423 | Highgate | 8 | TB | 8 | 2 add. ex R. 513/613 |
| 639 | Moorgate & Hampstead | ... | Sun. | 6 | 6 | 6 | 6 | 7256 | 433 | Highgate | 6 | TB | 6 | |

These items ar[e] from the 639 Ban[k] Holiday schedu[le] and the ordinar[y] schedule.

Finchley 609 has come 'a cropper' when passing under the section feeder just before Windsor Terrace; Finchley's breakdown tender 737J attends. The L3s nearside boom has got a nasty bend in it and some considerable time will be needed to straighten it. When repairs have finished, it will continue to Moorgate where the crew will be given instructions as to where they should go next.

*D.W.K. Jones*

Not having any bother in City Road is Finchley's 942 which has passed through the Windsor Terrace crossov
on 1st November 1958. Conductors working a '609 rounder' - Barnet/Moorgate/Barnet - had to pull seven fr
handles each time. Any Finchley duties that comprised three 609 'rounders' involved conductors jumping on a
off a trolleybus platform twenty-one times – good exercise though.                                    *John Clar*

J3 1044, a 611 to Moorgate, is outside Old Street station and about to pass under the City Road/Old Stre
overhead complex. Old Street is on the City branch of the Northern Line; there is just one entrance to it.
                                                                                                *Tony Belt*

inchley's 1457 has dewired in City Road just before the approach to Finsbury Square; this is on a straight stretch
f overhead so the reason for the poles leaving the wires is not known. A tower wagon attends the scene; two men
n its moveable tower attend to the booms. Once repairs have been completed 1457 will move round to its 609
Moorgate terminus.
*Don Lewis*

A smart looking 1425 has its front wheels on almost full lock as it turns from City Road into Finsbury Square. L3
425 works on route 639 - its destination blind has already been changed for the return trip to Hampstead Heath.
*Don Thompson*

This view taken on 27th Jur 1939 shows B3 491 in origin. livery with a silver ro which was red at each en 491 still has its original dee mudguards but no offsid route stencil. Upon deliver there was no immediate wor for the B3s so they were ser to Holloway depot and use whenever a need arose.

*Don Thompso*

London Transport wa under pressure by Finsbur Square businesses to us the least number of tractio standards as possible in th vicinity. Aesthetic reasor were probably quoted b it is more likely that thos occupying offices in the are did not want traction pole and overhead wires blightin the scene; maybe those wh worked at Royal Londo House were examples of th anti-trolleybus brigade. T keep the peace, span wire were fastened to rosettes on number of buildings, includin the one behind J1 913 which moving from the north to th east side of Finsbury Squar on 3rd April 1960. Highgat depot had not operated J1 until 11th November 195 when three ex-Finchle vehicles moved in. 913 arrive on 11th January 1961; it wi soon head to Parliament Hi Fields on route 615.

*Lyndon Row*

L2 1370 has just started it days' work on route 60 when it left Highgate depo the driver used the firs **MOORGATE** panel he cam across – for 615s/639s. He wi be partaking in a lot of blinc winding when he looks for hi next destination – Barnet o North Finchley. *Fred Ive*

L3 1460 on route 609 moves from the north side of Finsbury Square to the east side on 15th October 1960. It is about to pass under the single bowstring bracket arm on the east side of the square at the time.

*Peter Mitchell 16377*

L1 1360 on the 609 is in as-delivered condition; no offside route stencil is fitted so it shows a blank white panel. 1360's front advertisements state that the Northern Line was to be extended from Archway to East Finchley on 3rd July 1939 (confirming a 27th June 1939 date quoted for this view). Apart from a small amount of Sunday work by Finchley depot, Holloway operated the 609 daily from March 1938 until October 1941. The siding wire is available for vehicles to use.

*Don Thompson*

B2 103 running as 23 on route 615 is parked on the east side of Finsbury Square on a bright sunny 6th May 1948; so strong is the sun that the booms of the trolleybus in front cast a shadow on 103's front panel. 'BEN TRUMAN' reckon they have the best bottled beer; the car to the rear of 103 is registered LRT 1 which is a quite rare Armstrong Siddeley.

*James Aston*

Route 615 worked betwee
Moorgate and Parliame
Hill Fields; although som
trolleybus routes ha
alterations over the year
the 615 was not one of ther
Exemplifying three classes ar
C1 170, B3 484 and J2B 1007
Each has an item of note: 17
(with three vehicles behind i
has no front advertisement
484 had been a gener
runabout vehicle for mar
years and is first noted i
London Transport records o
20th August 1948 - allocate
to Holloway depot. Prior t
this it had been a permanen
training vehicle and also use
for miscellaneous purpose
it was pressed into servic
at Fulwell depot whe
required. 1007B is a rebodie
vehicle with its fleet numbe
digits very prominent. A
vehicles have linen route an
destination blinds.

*Fred Ive
Don Jone
Fred Ive*

L2 1377 waits out time on route 615 at Moorgate just before the second world war; the lay-by wire allows trolleybuses to pass each other when need be. Both sets of wires are fastened to the bowstring arm of a traction pole; in due course the inside set will be positioned further round the loop and supplied with a facing and trailing frog. 1377 is on the outside set of wires. The via point of Camden Town on the destination blind is for route 615 so is incorrect as this route does not pass through Camden Town. However, this description pertained through to the end of trolleybus blind manufacture at Holloway/Highgate on destination and side blinds. The correct description should have been **VIA CAMDEN ROAD.**                 *W. J. Haynes*

The east side of Finsbu[ry] Square often saw four or fi[ve] trolleybuses parked in line; [in] this view C3 332 leads thr[ee] others. 332 is working on o[ne] of the three evening peak ho[ur] trips that only went as far [as] **ARCHWAY STATION** [on] route 609. Staff working the[se] 'shorts' had to deal with eig[ht] frog pulls on each round trip: [1)] East Road/City Road, 2) Upp[er] Street/Essex Road, 3) Na[gs] Head, 4) Highgate-Archwa[y] 5) MacDonald Road, Archw[ay] 6) Holloway Road/Camde[n] Road, 7) Islington High Stre[et] 8) City Road/Goswell Roa[d] What an enjoyable part of [the] duty for conductors!

Finsbury Square at Moorga[te] could become very congeste[d] as shown in these two view[s] In the first image L3 143[9] on the 615 is the first [of] three trolleybuses and tw[o] Routemasters; L2 1374 [is] about to park up. In th[e] second view, a 609 make[s] it four in a row, impedin[g] departure of buses on route[s] 256/271. Excellent! *Don Lew[is]*

X5 1379 undertook some trips in the Kingsway tram subway on 13th August 1939 to test the feasibility of trolleybuses running through the tunnel; it was deemed unsuccessful and 1379 spent its whole life at Holloway/Highgate depot where it was normally seen on routes 627/653. For it to be allocated to the 615 is very unusual; 1379's rear end is very distinctive. It is 13th December 1952.

*Lyndon Rowe*

Routes 615 and 639 were withdrawn after operations on 31st January 1961; this view was taken three days earlier - on 28th January. Neither M1 1553 or K2 1334 are original Highgate stock; 1553 came from Bow in March 1955 with 1334 arriving from Lea Bridge in April 1959. The driver of 1334 has just got its trolley poles far enough beyond the facing frog to allow 1553 to pass. Vehicles using the outside wire needed the frog handle to be pulled down.

*A. G. Newman*

B2 131 is parked at the loading point at Moorgate sometime in 1948 awaiting its next trip to Hampstead Heath on route 639; behind is L1 1359 going to Highgate Village on the 611. The two routes part company at East Road in City Road.

*Alan Cross*

A second view of 1379 ⟨on⟩ route 615 on the same day ⟨as⟩ the previous view is show⟨n;⟩ it is now at the loadi⟨ng⟩ point. Apart from rout⟨es⟩ 513/611/613/639, photograph⟨s⟩ of this vehicle have been see⟨n⟩ on all of Highgate depo⟨t⟩ services. *Lyndon Row⟨⟩*

Route 609 commenced ⟨on⟩ Sunday 6th March 1938. Th⟨is⟩ view of Holloway's H1 759 wa⟨s⟩ probably taken that day; th⟨e⟩ number of bystanders impli⟨es⟩ this. At the time there wa⟨s⟩ just a single wire on the ea⟨st⟩ side of Finsbury Square; th⟨e⟩ traction pole in view is painte⟨d⟩ silver apart from a couple ⟨of⟩ feet of black paint at its bas⟨e.⟩ *Charles Klapp⟨er⟩*

J1 909 on route 609 is on th⟨e⟩ inside set of the Moorga⟨te⟩ wires sometime in 1948. A⟨ll⟩ blinds were made at Charlto⟨n⟩ Works at the time an⟨d⟩ therefore manufactured i⟨n⟩ linen. A bowstring bracket ar⟨m⟩ supports the two overhea⟨d⟩ tracks. *Alan Cro⟨⟩*

On the south side of Finsbury Square on route 615 are B2 120 and F1 750; both had initially been allocated to other depots. 120 spent its first four years at Bexleyheath with 750 being at Hanwell until 1955. The via point for Parliament Hill Fields is positioned differently on the two vehicles.          *Alan Cross/ S.N.J. White*

B3 486 on the 615 along with K2 1225 on route 683 wait out time at Finsbury Square sometime in 1948. Depot code plates are not in use yet– just running numbers. 486's conductor has yet to change the blind to show Parliament Hill Fields. There are many varied linen destination blind displays for routes 513/613/615/639 in this book – worth an intricate study by readers with an avid interest in blinds.          *Alan Cross*

# TIMES OF FIRST AND LAST TROLLEYBUSES

Route

## 609 - BARNET CHURCH AND MOORGATE

## 611 - HIGHGATE VILLAGE AND MOORGATE

## 615 - PARLIAMENT HILL FIELDS AND MOORGATE (VIA GREAT COLLEGE STREET)

## 639 - HAMPSTEAD AND MOORGATE (VIA CROWNDALE ROAD)

## 641 - WINCHMORE HILL AND MOORGATE

## 683 - STAMFORD HILL AND MOORGATE (WEEKDAYS ONLY)

| FROM | TO | MONDAY to FRIDAY | | SATURDAY | | SUNDAY | |
|---|---|---|---|---|---|---|---|
| | | First | Last | First | Last | First | Last |
| | | Morning | Night | Morning | Night | Morning | Night |
| Moorgate | Barnet Church ... | 6 9 | 11 0 | 6 9 | 11 29 | 8 11 | 10 52 |
| | North Finchley ... | 5 30 | 12 36 | 5 30 | 12 35 | 7 35 | 11 48 |
| | Highgate Village ... | 6 51 | 11 27 | 6 51 | 12 2 | 7 55 | 11 54 |
| | Highgate (Archway Tav.) ... | 5 30 | 12 36 | 5 30 | 12 35 | 6 35 | 12 36 |
| | Parliament Hill Fields ... | 7 3 | 11 44 | 7 3 | 11 30 | 9 36 | 11 45 |
| | Hampstead ... | 5 28 | 12 10 | 5 28 | 12 10 | 7 50 | 12 10 |
| | Winchmore Hill ... | 6 10 | 10 54 | 6 10 | 10 59 | 8 38 | 10 58 |
| | Wood Green Station (Und.) | { 5 0 / 5 50 / 6 10 | 12 32 | { 5 0 / 5 50 / 6 10 | 12 38 | { 6 53 / 7 49* / 8 38 | 12 35 |
| | Stamford Hill ... | 7 25 | 7 59 | 7 25 | 12 9 | — | — |
| Barnet Church | Moorgate ... ... | 5 39 | 11 39 | 5 39 | 11 32 | 9 13 | 11 36 |
| North Finchley (Tally Ho Corner) | Moorgate ... ... | 5 53 | 11 54 | 5 53 | 11 47 | 8 6 | 11 50 |
| Highgate Village | Moorgate ... ... | 7 8 | 11 22 | 7 8 | 11 54 | 7 21 | 11 46 |
| Highgate (Archway Tavern) | Moorgate ... ... | 5 0 | 12 10 | 5 0 | 12 5 | 6 8 | 12 8 |
| Parliament Hill Fields | Moorgate ... ... | 6 33 | 11 24 | 6 33 | 11 19 | 9 5 | 11 34 |
| Hampstead | Moorgate ... ... | 4 49 | 11 38 | 4 49 | 11 36 | 7 20 | 11 38 |
| Kings Cross | Moorgate ... ... | 5 5 | 11 54 | 5 5 | 11 52 | 7 35 | 11 53 |
| Winchmore Hill | Moorgate ... ... | 6 54 | 11 43 | 6 54 | 11 48 | 9 26 | 11 45 |
| Wood Green Stn. (Und.) | Moorgate ... ... | { 4 19 / 5 14 / 5 34 | 11 57 | { 4 19 / 5 14 / 5 34 | 12 3 | { 6 19 / 7 15 | 11 59 |
| Stamford Hill | Moorgate ... ... | 6 59 | 7 31 | 6 59 | 11 41 | — | — |

\* To Turnpike Lane only

## SERVICE INTERVALS

| BETWEEN | MONDAY to FRIDAY | | SATURDAY | | SUNDAY | |
|---|---|---|---|---|---|---|
| | Peak | Normal | Peak | Normal | Morn. | Evening |
| | Mins. | Mins. | Mins. | Mins. | Mins. | Mins. |
| Barnet Church and Moorgate ... ... ... | 6 | 8 | 6 | 6 | 8 | 8 |
| Barnet Church and Islington Green ... ... | 6 | 8 | 6 | 6 | 8 | 4 |
| Parliament Hill Fields and Moorgate... ... | 5 | 6 | 5 | 6 | 6 | 6 |
| Hampstead and Moorgate ... ... ... | 5 | 6 | 5 | 6 | 6 | 6 |
| Highgate Village and Moorgate ... ... | 4 | 6 | 4 | 6 | 5 | 8 |
| Winchmore Hill and Moorgate ... ... | 6 | 8 | 6 | 8 | 6 | 4 |
| Turnpike Lane and Moorgate ... ... ... | 3 | 4 | 3 | 4 | 6 | 4 |
| Stamford Hill and Moorgate ... ... ... | 5 | 5—10 | 5 | 8 | — | — |

ON PUBLIC HOLIDAYS services run at special times which are advertised on the vehicles

All enquiries to :—LONDON TRANSPORT, 55 BROADWAY, S.W.1
39/1157D-Proof  Post between Old Street and Moorgate
ABBey 1234
68
The Dangerfield Printing Co., Ltd., London.

On 21st June 1960, L3 1466 has just passed through the trailing frog at Moorgate and about to move from Finsbury Square into Finsbury Pavement. It is working on route 609 to Barnet, a journey that will take about an hour.

*Peter Mitchell 15297*

Moorgate tram terminus was at the bottom of Finsbury Pavement where E1 1061 is parked; it is going to route 9's peak hour terminus of Whetstone. It is the routes' last days as a poster about tram route 9 being replaced by trolleybus route 609 is positioned on its rocker panel. 1061 is also up for withdrawal.

*W.A. Camwell*

In Finsbury Pavement H1 799 is probably on its first day in service - 6th March 1938; it heads for Barnet on route 609. Transferred to Bexleyheath depot in 1939 its body was damaged beyond repair when BX was bombed on 29th June 1944; a new body saw it re-classified as H1B 799B on return from East Lancs Coachworks.

L3 1515 has not been pulle
into the side of the road t
pick up passengers at the fir
stop after leaving Moorga
on 6th September 1961 – ne
a dedicated member of sta
as the destination blind is ye
to be changed too. Route 6(
has two months and one da
more of life left. Bowstrir
bracket arms are in us
*Clarence Cart*

L2 1371 is working on rout
615 on 12th January 196
It moves through the OI
Street/City Road junction a
it heads to Parliament Hi
Fields.          *Denis Battan*

Exiting Windsor Terrac
loop and passing through it
crossover is a late-runnin
1045 which heads back t
Parliament Hill Fields o
route 615. Taken out c
service at stage seven of th
conversion scheme, J3 104
was reinstated to Highgat
depot nineteen days late
it was finally withdrawn a
stage nine of the programm
*Peter Moor*

1395 has been descending City Road but is now climbing it to cross the canal bridge over the City Road Basin by Wharf Road on Saturday 23rd July 1960 at 10.55am. The photographer continues his westbound pilgrimage and at 11am records L1 1356 at Hall Street. Both trolleybuses head for Moorgate on route 615.
*Peter Mitchell 15562/15563*

### CITY ROAD, NEAR "ANGEL" JUNCTION.

Frog is situated at Pole No. 81, City Road.   Two push buttons are fixed on Pole No. 81 :—
Upper button for High Street, Islington.
Lower button for Pentonville Road.
Frog is normally set for High Street, Islington, and is automatically re-set for High Street after operation.
Indicator on Pole No. 82 shews direction for which frog is set, thus :—

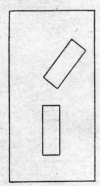

*Set for
High Street, Islington.*

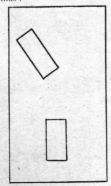

*Set for
Pentonville Road.*

In event of failure of electrical apparatus :—
Pull down for Pentonville Road.
Push up for High Street.

This and the following view were taken on 31st December 1960. L3 1525 is on the nearside set of wires that will take it down Pentonville Road on route 639 to Hampstead Heath. The pointer arm on the box on the traction standard on the left shows that 609s do not require a frog pull here.

*John Gillham*

The photographer then moves to the top of Goswell Road where there are two dead-end sets of wires - they are remnants of route 677 which was withdrawn after operations on 14th April 1957. The left-hand wires which took 677s towards Hackney are tied off against a traction pole; the wires in the centre were for Smithfield. The Goswell Road wires are still energised and will be for another four months and two weeks. They were retained for emergency use in case there was a problem with 679s in St John Street; this did not occur and they were unused for over two years.

*John Gillham*

Almost at the top of City Road L3 1447 has stopped for passengers to board and alight; this is also where 609s diverge from 615s/639s. In this instance, 1447 working to Hampstead Heath on route 639 on 21st January 1961, needs to access the left-hand set of wires. On 1447's platform a conductor is undergoing training – maybe the regular conductor (who is pulling the semi-automatic frog handle) feels it is better that he activates this piece of equipment to save any mishap. The three trolleybus services that operate in City Road each have an E plate in the bus stop E plate holder. The canvas hut provides protection from the elements for a light duty man who at busy times would pull the frog handle down, thus speeding 615s/639s on their way – the hut also had a rudimentary seat for him.

*Hugh Taylor*

This view was taken at the junction of Goswell Road with City Road on a wet 29th January 1961 with MI 1553 having passed the traffic lights. It is working on route 615 to Parliament Hill Fields; according to the clock in the centre of the picture it is 2.59pm.          *Tony Belton*

At the City Road/Islington High Street/St John Street junction, 1380 - the first L3 and the only London trolleybus to carry an FXF registration - has been allocated to route 609 one Sunday and heads for North Finchley. A lack of advertisers sees 'stock labels' being used on its front panels.          *Fred Ivey*

At the same place as the previous view, J2 1002 heads across the junction on its way to Parliament Hill Fields on route 615. The remaining J2s at Highgate depot were exchanged for L3s from West Ham at stage six of the conversion scheme; the L3s only lasted nine months there as most were forwarded to Fulwell depot at stage nine of the conversion programme.          *Michael Dryhurst*

A busy scene at 'Angel Junction' on 31st December 1960 sees L3 1382 entering City Road while working on route 615 to Moorgate; going the other way a 'roof-box' R is heading to Finsbury Park on route 4. The traffic light signal is on amber; attached to the signals is a very large NO RIGHT TURN sign - this tells motorists they cannot turn from Pentonville Road into St John Street.              *Jack Greaves*

Looking the other way Mr Gillham has, in two views, captured all the 'special work' where 615s/639s meet 609s/679s at 'Angel'. On the back of these photos, he wrote in pencil: ANGEL ISLINGTON PENTONVILLE ROAD LK WEST 31 DEC 60.
                    *John Gillham*

Highgate depot had a small number of K class vehicles allocated over the years; K1 1267 moved in from Clapton depot in May 1955. It is at the top of Pentonville Road on the approach to 'The Angel' Islington on 23rd July 1960; it operates on route 615 to Moorgate.

*Peter Mitchell 15564*

These views were taken at almost the top of the incline in Pentonville Road; the first image on 19th February 1949 shows B2 121 working on route 615 to **PARLIAMENT** – the conductor has made a poor job of showing what should be **PARLIAMENT HILL FIELDS.** Many years later, with a much-altered background, K1 1062 has its blinds set properly for Hampstead Heath on route 639.

*Alan Cross/Michael Dryhurst*

Climbing Pentonville Road with ease M1 1537 heads for Moorgate on the 615 on 23rd July 1960. The M1s wer
scheduled for withdrawal in April 1960; due to vehicles of various classes falling by the wayside, eight stayed i
service until November 1961.
*Peter Mitchell 1556*

Going down the hill in Pentonville Road and past Kings Cross coach station M1B 1543B heads for Hampstea
Heath on the 639. A short way further back is Penton Street where the Public Carriage Office was situated; thi
was where trolleybus conductors' and drivers' licences were issued and renewed.
*Michael Dryhurs*

The Kings Cross Road/ Pentonville Road overhead layout on 31st December 1960; the routes illustrated here were not all that frequent so it unusual to see four trolleybuses together. Top) 1395 is on route 639; in the centre is 1382 on the 615 with another vehicle behind; 1427 on route 513 is to the right. In early trolleybus years route 613 travelled along Kings Cross Road on its way to Holborn Circus. Lower) Looking in the opposite direction is the view from the east. Intriguingly, Mr Gillham and Mr Gready are photographing London trolleybuses on the same day at the same place.

*Jack Gready/ John Gillham*

Caledonian Road is off to the right. L3 1384 is only going to **WINDSOR TERRACE CITY ROAD** on the 639; there is a lot of traffic around so it has been delayed on its trip to Moorgate and is therefore curtailed. A lot of 'special work' is aloft here so drivers need to use all their skill to get through the frogs and crossings without getting stuck on 'dead' sections. Out of necessity, two short traction poles are placed on the roof of a shop on the left - one is in view.

*Tony Belton*

At the lower end of Pentonville Road, the first K1 - 1055 - headed for Parliament Hill Fields on the 513. It arrived at Highgate depot in January 1953; it recorded by London Transport as transferred to Wood Green on 27th April 1960 and then to Isleworth depot on 26th April 1961. It is a hot day as both front windscreens are open.
*Anthony Wright*

N1 1606 - a refugee from Walthamstow depot in February 1960 - is working on route 639 to Hampstead Heath. It is at the bottom of Pentonville Road with York Way to the immediate left.
*Fred Ivey*

This view was taken in Kings Cross, with 127 crossing from Pentonville Road into Euston Road. B2 127 is working the Parliament Hill Fields on the 513; although the route number is clean the same cannot be said for the well used destination blind.
*Jim Wyndham*

At the same place as the previous view but on 31st December 1960 two trolleybuses are adjacent to each other. However, L3 1391 on the 615 has dewired; L2 1378 which is a 639 to Hampstead Heath waits for the situation to be rectified.
*John Gillham*

In Euston Road and heading for Highgate depot on route 513, J2B 993B has few passengers on board; the last alighting place will be by JUNCTION ROAD MONNERY ROAD. Apart from a stint at Finchley between February 1957 and November 1959 this rebodied vehicle (formerly J2 993) spent its entire life at Holloway/Highgate depot.
*Fred Ivey*

N1 1581 is on its way to Hampstead Heath on route 639 on 11th December 1960. There is no mistaking where this photograph was taken; the edifice in the background states the obvious: BRITISH RAILWAYS KINGS CROSS.
*Lyndon Rowe*

K1 1061 on route 615 is in Euston Road but only going as far as Kings Cross; it will make its way to Grays Inn Road and thence to Swinton Street where it terminates - at departure time it will travel along Kings Cross Road and into Pentonville Road to pick up line of route. 1061 was allocated to Edmonton depot from new in October 1938 with a move to Hanwell occurring in the early part of the war. It returned to north London in March 1955, going to Highgate depot; stage two of the conversion scheme saw it go to Wood Green in April 1959. A return to Highgate occurred three months later. Back to Wood Green at stage six - April 1960; at stage twelve it was withdrawn and sent to Isleworth on 8th November 1961 as a Rolling Stock Engineer's spare vehicle. Its next stock number up, 1062, was hit up the back in early February 1962 so 1061 was reinstated and in doing so became the last London trolleybus to be relicensed – on 7th February 1962. What a merry-go-round for 1061. A

74

H1 783 was delivered to London Transport in January 1938 and sent to Holloway depot in March 1938, moving to Wood Green depot on 1st June 1938. It remained at WN for the rest of its life. However, on the day this photograph was taken it was on loan to Highgate where it works as HT 9 on route 613; it turns from Euston Road into Pancras Road. The destination blind does not sit well behind the glass of the box as 783 has a reduced depth blind fitted. The driver has failed to change the blind to show Hampstead Heath and has run all the way from Holborn Circus without it being brought to his attention.

*Fred Ivey*

75

For some reason B2 126, a 639 to Hampstead Heath, is parked with its poles down opposite Kings Cross station in the early post-war period; passengers wait patiently for their journeys to continue. For about a hundred yards trolleybuses travelled along Euston Road in both directions.
*V.C. Jones*

The photographer found a viewing point over the highway so that L3 1453 is seen from above; it enters Pancras Road while working on the 613 to Hampstead Heath. The image shows trolley gantry, trolley base and trolley arms of a London trolleybus; the wooden gang-plank allows staff to work on roof-mounted equipment. *Fred Ivey*

It is 13th July 1939 and J2 992 is just over a year old; it is at the southern end of Pancras Road at Kings Cross. The destination blind panel is the first of many provided over the years for 615s to show Moorgate; this one is very informative and has been perfectly set by the driver. London Transport are using trolleybus advertisement panels to promote their **GREEN LINE** services.

*Geoff Pearce*

| 615 | Parliament Hill Fields (clockwise) |
|---|---|
| | Highgate Road/Fortess Road (clockwise) |
| | City Road |
| | *(1) Macclesfield Road (clockwise) battery |
| | (2) Windsor Terrace (clockwise) Bank holidays, summer Sundays and * |
| | Finsbury Square (clockwise) |

This curtailment instruction for route 615 does not list Kings Cross despite there being many scheduled turns there.

At the lower end of Pancras Road on 13th July 1939, J2 1022 on the 639 and L1 1366 on route 615 are photographed. This is a crew changeover point; in later years these mostly took place at Fortess Walk in Kentish Town. White dustcoats for drivers were standard issue at the time.

*Geoff Pearce*

| No. | Shew |
|---|---|
| | Front and Rear Blind. |
| 11 | Hampstead Heath via Camden Town |
| 13 | Via Kings Cross and Grays Inn Road, Holborn Circus |
| 15 | Via Kentish Town, Parliament Hill Fields |
| 14 | Holborn Circus via Kings Cross and Farringdon Street |
| 12 | Via Camden Town and Kings Cross, Moorgate |
| 15 | Via Kentish Town, Parliament Hill Fields |
| 12 | Via Camden Town and Kings Cross, Moorgate |
| 11 | Hampstead Heath via Camden Town |
| 11 | Hampstead Heath |
| 4 | Holloway Depot |

Panel 12 is shown twice - the 615 instruction shows that the 615 travels via Camden Town which is erroneous as it travels by Camden Road. The 639 entry is correct.

At the southern end of Pancras Road on 22nd September 1952, J2 988 and C1 132 head for Holborn Circus o
routes 513 and 613 respectively; both have linen blinds in their front boxes. 988 is without front adverts; 132's fror
adverts are for Tetley tea. 132's destination blind erroneously describes the via point of **FARRINGDON RD** a
**FARRINGDON ST**; this was an error created at Charlton Works on Holloway depot tram blinds and perpetuate
onto their trolleybus blinds for a number of years. 132 is the lowest numbered C1. Its original front lights are sti
in use and are seen in the cream band above the windscreen. This vehicle was sold to Penang, Malaysia in 195
Part of the St Pancras station complex is in the background.

*Alan Cro*

At the same place and same date as the previous two views, C1 137 and B2 116 head for Holborn Circus on the 513 nd 613 respectively. The destination blind panels for Holborn Circus on these vehicles should be compared with hose on the opposite page. Highgate depot are still using destination blinds made for vehicles that predominantly perated on the Hampstead routes. At present, short and long wheelbase vehicles work alongside each other on hese services. 137 has new sidelights built into its front dash but still retains its original high sidelights which are ow not used. 116 has new torpedo lights on each side of the front lower panels.                    *Alan Cross*

Seen outside St Pancras Station buildings in Pancras Road C1 161 heads for Hampstead Heath on the 639. All blinds on C1s were changed by the conductor. This vehicle has two sets of front lights - it is the lower set that are in use.
*John L. Smith*

In 1954/55 five N2s moved from Bow to Highgate depot which saw them working in areas in which they had not been seen before. Two were 1648 and 1650 which are at the bottom of Pancras Road working on route 639. Both ended up at Stonebridge depot where they remained serviceable until 2nd January 1962; they were not picked up by the scrapman until 21st March 1962 by which time they were in a very forlorn state.
*Michael Baker*

Some of the areas covered in this book are insalubrious as evidenced by J2 985 passing along Pancras Road on its way to Moorgate on route 639. To the left is one of the walls of St Pancras Railway Station which needs a major spruce-up.

Between 1955 and 1959 Highgate had some F1s on their books. 748 is by Wellers Court in Pancras Road on the 615 on 17th August 1958 but only going to Kings Cross. The surrounding area is known Somers Town.

*Peter Mitchell 11710*

At the top of Pancras Road N1 1565A works as a 513 to Holborn Circus; in the background a sign points to St Pancras Goods Station. 1565A had been 1565 whose body was destroyed in September 1940 when working out of Bow depot. *Fred Ivey*

These two views in Pancr
Road were taken underneat
the railway bridges where lin
led in and out of St Pancr
main line station. M1 1547
a 639 to Hampstead Heath;
has halted at the Phoenix Ro
traffic lights on 1st Januar
1961. Note the long piece
conductive metal betwee
the two bridges (fixed bot
ways). Starting away from th
same set of traffic lights M1
1543B heads to Parliamer
Hill Fields on the 513 on 1
November 1958.

*Denis Battams/John Clar*

Passing under the Somer
Town railway bridges tha
take railway lines into and ou
of Somers Town goods dep
is M1 1540 which is operatir
on route 615 to Moorga
on 1st January 1961. It ha
moved from West Ham t
Highgate depot in April 196
being further transferred t
Finchley in April 1961. Somer
Town was one of the drearie
places on the Londo
trolleybus network.

*Tony Belto*

1382 has passed under all of the Somers Town railway bridges and is now out in the open in Pancras Road while working on route 615 to Parliament Hill Fields on 29th January 1961. Most of Highgate's L3s were transferred to Fulwell depot at stage nine of the conversion scheme – not 1382 though as it was one of two members of the class withdrawn at the time. The bus stop flag adjacent to 1382 has a sticker affixed - it indicates that there will not be a stop at this location after 31st January; maybe few people boarded and alighted here so it could be dispensed with. *Peter Mitchell 16664*

Railway arches were a good source of revenue for British Railways. The arches were beneath the railway coal drops and were all occupied by coal merchants. J2 1000 on route 615 and L1 1369 on the 613 pass by. Number 1000 was the only trolleybus to have an **EXX** registration - **EXX 10**. *Fred Ivey/Alan Cross*

J3 1052 is in Pancras Road Somers Town on 17th August 1958. The J3s were ordered for route 611; however there was always a surplus of 'Highgate Hill' trolleybuses so it was common to see 1052 working on route 615 to Moorgate. 1426 on the 513 follows behind.

*Peter Mitchell 1170*

## 1915.—OVERHEAD POINTS AND FROGS—ROUTES Nos. 513, 613, 615 AND 639.

Notice to Drivers and Conductors.

CITY ROAD AT POLE No. 81, DOWN.

> Set for High Street, Islington.
> Pull for Hampstead and Parliament Hill.

KING'S CROSS ROAD AT POLE No. 239, DOWN.

> Set for Caledonian Road.
> Pull for Hampstead and Parliament Hill.

PENTONVILLE ROAD, KING'S CROSS ROAD AT POLE No. 31, UP.

> Set for City Road.
> Pull for King's Cross Road.

GRAYS INN ROAD, DERBY STREET, AT POLE No. 99, DOWN.

> Set for Caledonian Road.
> Pull for Hampstead and Parliament Hill.

EUSTON ROAD, YORK ROAD AT POLE No. 45, UP.

> Set for Pentonville Road.
> Pull for Grays Inn Road.

PANCRAS ROAD, GREAT COLLEGE STREET AT POLE No. 84, DOWN.

> Set for Great College Street.
> Pull for Crowndale Road.

Top) This view taken on 27th December 1960 is at the Crowndale Road/Royal College Street junction; conductors pull a semi-automatic frog handle for 639s to access Crowndale Road. Also seen is the trailing frog from Royal College Street into Pancras Road. Middle) L3 1441 passes by in the same direction while working on route 639 to Moorgate on 1st January 1961. Prominent is the signal box which indicates to drivers which way the frog is set – in this instance the illuminated 'Y' informs them that priority is for Royal College Street. 'The College Arms' sells Courage and Barclay beers etc. to those who enter. Below) Going the other way on the 615 on 18th January 1961, L3 1389 moves into Royal College Street.

*John Gillham/*
*Denis Battams/*
*Clarence Carter*

Seen in the same place as the previous view, E class tramcar 538 works on route 5; the three-line blind requires a extra-large destination box - it states that it travels to **HAMPSTEAD** CHALK FARM RD & KINGS CROSS. 538 in conduit mode; the motorman changes the points by hand to access Great College Street.

Moving from Royal College Street into Pancras Road 1437 heads for Holborn Circus on the 613. L3 1437 was a Highgate depot from 27th April 1960 until 31st January 1961, just three conversion stages. On the latter date moved to Fulwell where it stayed for fifteen months.

*Don Thompson*

What is now Royal College Street was originally Great College Street as shown by the name-plate on the building on the left; 124 is seen in the summer of 1939, shortly after transfer from Bexleyheath depot. This enabled Holloway's seventy-seater H1s to move to Bexleyheath where better use was made of them in the Woolwich area. The sixty-seater B2s coming the other way easily handled the lower amount of passenger traffic on the Hampstead routes. 124's side blind has been wound up almost as far as it can go and shows HOLBORN CIRCUS; this is unusual as it is displaying the terminal point of either route 513/613 – normally the side blind just showed via points. It cannot be ascertained which route 124 is working on as a plate is not fitted to the stencil holder to the side of the platform. Other items of interest are two belisha beacons and tram tracks still in-situ; they were last used on 9th July 1938. B2 124 retains its silver roof and original deep mudguards.

*London Transport Museum U12684*

On 6th August 1960, L3 1443 is by Pratt Street which is a road off Royal College Street. In the far background are the Camden Road railway bridges, distinctive landmarks in the area. 1443 operates on the 615 to Moorgate.

*Peter Mitchell 15720*

This is where Royal College Street crosses Camden Road heading for Moorgate on the 615 is J2 1019. In the first view both booms are on the wires; a few seconds later they have dewired when leaving the bridge on 18th April 1960. Not succumbing is L 1375 on its way to Holborn Circus on route 513 on 23rd June 1959. The Camden Road southbound wires cross the Royal College Street wires in normal fashion; the other three crossovers are in troughing under the bridge.

*Clarence Carter x 2*
*John Clarke*

1391 on the 613 to Holborn Circus is in Royal College Street just before it crosses Camden Road - it is 31st January 1961, the last day of the route. 'Close poling' it is 1383 which is only going to Kings Cross on the 513. In the evening, both will make a long trek to Fulwell depot where they will be working next day. *Peter Mitchell 16683*

Further up Royal College Street is one of Highgate's longstanding residents - 1023 which is working a trip to Parliament Hill Fields on route 615. J2 1023 is very close to the entrance of the long disused South Kentish Town underground station of the Northern Line.
*Fred Ivey*

Crowndale Road is a street in London where there was little of interest; of note though was the Working Men
College seen on the left. L1 1364 operates on the 639 to Hampstead Heath on 6th August 1960.

*Peter Mitchell 157*

Peter Mitchell is renowned for his first-class photography; with 1023 'dead centre' and strong sunlight this is th
result on 17th August 1958. J2 1023 operates on route 639 to Moorgate and is in Crowndale Road, a short wa
from Mornington Crescent.

*Peter Mitchell 117*

Just north of Camden Road Bridge L3 1414 without any front advertisements is working on route 653 to **TOTTENHAM CT RD**. This view was taken prior to the end of 1950 when Highgate put depot code plates and new style running numbers on their vehicles; it was the last depot to do this despite the feature generally appearing from October 1950. *S.N.J. White*

This photograph was taken shortly before stage ten of the conversion programme took place. Edmonton depot's K1 1084, working on route 627 to Tottenham Court Road, has just passed under one of the heavy Camden Road railway bridges (under which is the third example of a crossover without any other 'special work' illustrated in this book). British Railways inform 'one and all' that they provide frequent electric trains to a number of London suburbs. The amount of traffic in Camden Road shows how difficult it was for Central Road Services to keep bus and trolleybus services at regular service levels. Apart from some weekday peak hour work on the 627 by Wood Green depot the route was operated on an almost two-to-one basis (Highgate versus Edmonton). **FERODO BRAKE LININGS** are prominently advertised.

*Fred Ivey*

1574 was allocated to Highgate depot in January 1959; it works to Tottenham Court Road on the 627 and is adjacent to RTL 664 on the 29. N1 1574's driver will be confident he can get away from the traffic lights at Camden Street quicker than the RTL as they tended to be sluggish when starting from stationary. *Tony Belton*

Camden Town Station and buildings in the vicinity suffered bomb damage on the night of 14th/15th October 194
A traction pole has been temporarily replaced by the fitting of two rosettes anchored to the wall of a buildin
A section insulator has been inserted between two sets of cables feeding the overhead; it was a Board of Trad
requirement that power supplies had to be insulated at half mile sections (not all were at feeder locations
*London Transport Museum U2345*

C1 147 was allocated to Hounslow depot in October 1935; for the next seventeen years it did little else than wor
between Hounslow and Shepherds Bush on route 657. With the arrival of Q1s at what was now named Islewort
depot 147 moved to Highgate in October 1952. It was withdrawn in March 1955 having done nothing more tha
operate on the Hampstead routes. It is at Camden Town, working on route 639 to Moorgate; a rebuilt Camde
Town station is in the background.
*Alan Cros*

1554 on the 653 leads N1 1560 on the 627 through Camden Town on 7th January 1961. Both had been stablemates at Bow depot but due to reductions in service levels were transferred to Highgate – 1554 in March 1955 and 1560 in January 1959. L3 1398, formerly of West Ham, passes through the same crossover on route 639 on the same day - a reunion of 'East-enders' at this location! In the background is a branch of the Midland Bank which intriguingly has an UndergrounD roundel fixed to the top of it.

*Jack Gready*

J2 1006 is in Camden Town on 18th April 1960 heading for Hampstead Heath on the 639 at the same place on 23rd June 1959, J3 1052 is working on the 653 but only as far as Mile End Gate. There is plenty of traffic in both views but it does not appear to delay services.

*Clarence Carter*
*John Clark*

New overhead is in position and is being used in this view taken between July and November 1938 in Camden Town; apparent is the facing frog that takes 639s towards Hampstead Heath or 629s towards Holloway. To the rear is STL 420 working on route 63 to Chalk Farm. Ex-Walthamstow car 2055 is operating on route 27 to EDMONTON TN HALL; a tram on route 53 is in front of it.

Route 625 does not travel to **Tottenham Court Road!** A rare mistake by a member of staff. It should read routes 627, 629 and 641

## 629 nominated turning arrangements

| 629 | Enfield Town (clockwise) |
|---|---|
| | *Enfield, Bush Hill Park (clockwise) battery |
| | Winchmore Hill (clockwise) |
| | Palmers Green, Hoppers Road (clockwise) |
| | Wood Green Station (clockwise) |
| | Turnpike Lane Station (anti-clockwise) from south only |
| | †Manor House Station (clockwise) |
| | Finsbury Park, Coleridge Road (anti-clockwise) |
| | Holloway, Warlters Road (clockwise) before 7.30 a.m.: after 7.0 p.m. and * |
| | Mornington Crescent (clockwise) |
| | Tottenham Court Road |
| | Maple Street (clockwise) |

Saturday, 26th August, 1950.

    5.12 p.m. Camden Town Substation.  No. 2 Rectifier Transformer failed and tripped both H.T. feeders.

                    8 mins Passenger Delay.
                   16  "    Electrical  "
    (See also Railway Power Services)

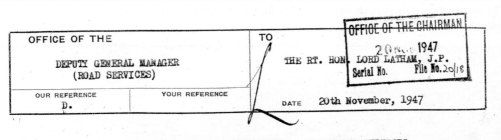

| OFFICE OF THE | | TO | OFFICE OF THE CHAIRMAN |
|---|---|---|---|
| DEPUTY GENERAL MANAGER (ROAD SERVICES) | | THE RT. HON. LORD LATHAM, J.P. | 20 NOV 1947 Serial No.    File No. 20/18 |
| OUR REFERENCE D. | YOUR REFERENCE | DATE 20th November, 1947 | |

INTERRUPTION OF POWER SUPPLY – TROLLEYBUS SERVICES
20th NOVEMBER, 1947

    Owing to the failure of the water supply to the Camden Town Railway Sub-Station, power was cut off from 7.43 to 8.50 this morning on the sections of the trolleybus system fed by this Sub-Station.  As a result trolleybus services were interrupted during this period between the following points:-

    Tottenham Court Road Terminus and Malden Road, Hampstead
    Crowndale Road, Royal College Street and Malden Road
    Crowndale Road and Camden Road

    The following routes were affected –

            513         629
            613         639
            627         653

DW.

610/3  (1)—X
(150m, 3/47—Stock)

| Sun. 2.7.44 | |
|---|---|
| 12.16 | Hammersmith. Windows of Trolleybus Depot damaged by blast. |
| 12.45 | Rochester Place, Camden Town. Three trolleybuses, Nos. 839, 824 and 843 on route 629, and No. 1378 on route 653 - windows damaged by blast. |

K1 1286 passes through Mornington Crescent on 7th January 1961 while working on route 629 to Enfield; it is a murky day with the Cobden statue only just being able to be made out. However, the semi-automatic frog hand and 'electric Y pointer' show up well; the frog is set for Tottenham Court Road. Route 639 and shortworking 627s/629s/653s needed conductors to operate this piece of equipment; 'shortworkers' needed another frog pull to access the loop there.

*Jack Gread*

K1 1296 on the 629 has entered **MORNINGTON CRESCENT STN** shortworking loop in the run-up to stage te of the conversion scheme; this is deduced by the fact that not only does 1296 have a painted depot code but also that the advertisement for 'The Greatest Show on Earth' was initially shown in 1961. In the foreground a coupl of street loungers lean and sit on railings.

*Derek Norma*

There were times when 653s were scheduled to turn at Mornington Crescent Station. M1 1541 is running as HT139 which has just despatched a middle-aged couple into the roadway as parked cars prevent them getting onto the pavement. The conductor is probably at the frog handle ready to pull it down to allow 1541 onto the loop.

Also turning at **MORNINGTON CRES STATION** is Edmonton's K3 1677. Although 627s did not operate on Sundays it did on Bank Holiday Mondays (when this photo was taken) so that staff who would otherwise be unoccupied were working. *Don Thompson*

Having taken the left-hand wiring at Mornington Crescent F1 749 is about to turn left into Crowndale Road while working on route 639 to Moorgate on 22nd May 1955; this vehicle had only been at Highgate depot for eighteen days, having arrived on 4th May. The frog under which 749 is about to pass is for trolleybuses turning short here. Cobden statue is prominent in this view.
*Don Thompson*

L3 1380, has just passe[d] through the trailing fro[g] outside Mornington Crescen[t] Station on 7th January 196[?] shortworking vehicles stoo[d] on what is seen here as th[e] right-hand wire. 1380, a 63[9] to Hampstead Heath, will no[w] pass through the crossove[r] that takes trolleybuses t[o] Tottenham Court Road.

*Jack Gread*

Some Sunday evening turn[s] on route 653 were made a[t] Mornington Crescent Statio[n] why they were provided is no[t] known. L1 1357 illustrates thi[s] at 7.13pm on 3rd July 196[0]

*Peter Mitchell 1539*

M1 1553 leaves Morningto[n] Crescent loop on a schedule[d] These 'shorts' were provide[d] because trolleybuses coul[d] arrive full from Tottenha[m] Court Road, causing passenge[r] delays here. Morningto[n] Crescent Station has a[n] impressive frontage. *Fred Ive[?]*

98

Route 639 has been withdrawn as there is just a single loop outside Mornington Crescent Station now – wiring down Crowndale Road had been removed by the time the top image was taken on 16th March 1961. Wood Green depot is still training men to the role of trolleybus driver with 1294 used on this occasion. The instructor has ensured that the side and route blind panels are turned to the white aperture at the top of the blinds. **PRIVATE** is shown at the front (no doubt the appropriate panels are displayed at the rear). In the second view, taken on 20th April 1961, K1 1294 is on Mornington Crescent loop and returning to Wood Green depot on route 629; in the meantime, the front advertisements have changed. 1294 in training and service mode on the same shortworking loop: well done, Denis. *Denis Battams*

The final piece of equipment to be illustrated at this location is the northbound trailing frog. On 27th December 1960 what is thought to be K2 1352 moves along Camden High Street towards Camden Town with a learner trolleybus in front of it. *John Gillham*

Outside Mornington Crescent station N1 1574 is working the full length of route 627 to Waltham Cross. Heading towards Tottenham Court Road is Wood Green's 1058 on the 629. The advert fixer at Highgate depot is not someone who pays attention to detail as the front adverts have been fixed the wrong way round. 1574 should be showing 'See and be seen'.

*Tony Belton*

Approaching Mornington Crescent during its stay at Wood Green depot, K2 1253 is running late on route 629 and has been curtailed to Winchmore Hill. When Mr Ivey took this photograph, he would have had no idea that upon withdrawal at stage ten of the conversion scheme 1253 would survive the scrapping cull; a bright future awaited and it became part of London Transport's Museum collection.

*Fred Ivey*

| Fri. 25.2.44 00.55 | NORTHERN CONTROLLER (TROLLEYBUSES) reports:- Incident at Mornington Crescent, Hampstead Road. Incendiary bomb dropped and broke a sidelight and twisted the trolleyhead of Trolleybus No. 774, Service 629; also brought the positive wire down. |
| --- | --- |

K2 1311 is in Hampstead Road, just south of Mornington Crescent, on 5th March 1961 while working on route 629 to **TOTTENHAM COURT RD.** The building on the left is occupied by **CARRERAS** which is the head office of a tobacco distribution centre; many a 629 crew and passenger will unknowingly have bought products they organise or despatch.

*Peter Mitchell 16826*

J1 922 worked from Finchley depot between 6th March 1938 and 10th November 1959 when it was delicensed; with vehicles falling by the wayside at Highgate shortly afterwards, 922 was sent to HT. This reinstatement commenced on 23rd November 1959 and concluded on 27th April 1960, the longest time span of a J1 at Highgate. 922 is on the 653 and in Hampstead Road, just south of the previous image.

*Michael Dryhurst*

Another N1 passing to Highgate in January 1959 was 1577 which is in Hampstead Road passing Drummond Street on 8th January 1961. It has been working at HT for two years now; in this instance it is a 653 to Tottenham Court Road.                                                                                                                           *Peter Mitchell 1657*

Tram routes 27, 29 and 53 terminated at the junction of Euston Road with Hampstead Road which London Transport considered to be its Tottenham Court Road tram terminus. E1 1108 is resting from its labours; its next trip is to Aldgate – the 53 was colloquially known as the 'bagels' route due to its circular nature.        *W. A. Camwell*

Directly outside Warren Street station N2 1668 is only going to Edmonton Town Hall. There was no passenger traffic need for all 627s to go to Waltham Cross, hence the shortworking.

*Tony Belton*

103

K1 1059 was immediatel recognisable to the latter-day Londo trolleybus enthusiast; it sported wire grille which was probably fitte in lieu of its ordinary one when was at Hanwell depot many year earlier. Now at Wood Green depo it is not far from the 629's souther terminus of Tottenham Court Roa In the background is a branch of th Westminster bank; affixed to a po is an impressive sign for EUSTO SQUARE STATION. It is 5th Marc 1961.          *Peter Mitchell 1683*

It is the last day that trolleybuse operate in Tottenham Cour Road (25th April 1961) and th photographer is sitting in th upstairs front offside seat of northbound trolleybus. Bunching c 627s was frequent with Highgate 1577 and Edmonton's 1231 bein the offenders as they near the end c their southbound trips; just in view i an RT on route 134. Maples store i on the right.          *Brian Spelle*

Trolleybuses travelled clockwis around Tottenham Court Roa loop; an alternative set of wirin was constructed for anti-clockwis movement at the request of th police. A uniquely constructe traction pole (number 32) with bowstring arm fixed each side wa positioned in Tottenham Court Roa - between Maple Street and Howlan Street. JCG describes this piece c equipment as CENTRE POLE DOUBLE BRACKET ARM whic shows up well in this view of L2 137 on 11th March 1961, the day after i reinstatement to Highgate depo The driver has already change 1372's blind to show Waltham Cro where this 627 will terminate on i next journey.          *John Gillha*

K1 1291 turns from Tottenham Court Road into Howland Street while working on route 629 on 15th April 1961; within a fortnight 1291 would be parked up in Isleworth depot, awaiting a return to service – this occurred on 13th July. The wiring in the other direction was only used in emergencies.
*Ray Golds*

London Transport were hoping to extend their new trolleybus services beyond Euston as far as Bedford Square (not all that far from Oxford Street) but were thwarted by objections from various organisations and authorities. The furthest south they were allowed to go was Howland Street into which road K2 1317, on route 653, is turning; an RTL on route 73 heads south. If London Transport had got their way, trolleybus wires would have extended south from this point.

In Howland Street, K1 1138 on route 653 is parked at the bus stop there. The anti-clockwise wiring leading from Howland Street back into Tottenham Court Road is also seen.
*Alan Cross*

Stand time for trolleybuses at Tottenham Court Road terminus was supposed to be taken in Maple Street; however, on 2nd August 1952 the drivers of L3s 1418 and 1419 have parked in Howland Street, the first of three roads used here. Both will move round to Maple Street in due course. 1418 will probably end its next trip on route 653 at Aldgate while 1419 will go to Edmonton Town Hall on the 627. In each view another trolleybus is parked further down Howland Street - maybe staff have been instructed to do this for some reason. Neither vehicle has front advertisements fitted.

*Peter Grace*

K2 1253 is almost at the end of a journey to Tottenham Court Road on route 629 on 11th March 1961. The wires coming in from the left are from Whitfield Street and form part of the anti-clockwise loop which was constructed at the insistence of the police; back in 1938, they were concerned about 'trolleybus congestion' here so London Transport had to comply. *John Gillham*

Moving from Howland Street into Fitzroy Street is J2 1022 on route 627; the driver has already changed the destination blind to show **EDMONTON TOWN HALL**. Part of the destination glass is masked to accommodate reduced depth blinds at Highgate depot; when full size blinds were used this was the result. *Alan Cross*

Three traction poles with single bracket arms were erected in Fitzroy Street; traction standards were normally positioned on the nearside where one-way wiring was used but in this case are placed on the offside with five being bent beneath ground to avoid obstruction. K1 1055 on the 629 is in view when this picture was taken on 11th March 1961. *John Gillham*

At the top of Howland Street and turning into Fitzroy Street is N1A 1587A, working on route 653 to Aldgate; 1587A spent six years at Highgate depot (1952-1958). It would pass to Stonebridge and then Finchley depot, being withdrawn in November 1959; it was the last Weymann re-bodied vehicle in service.

*John Clarke*

| Fri. 30.6.44 | | |
|---|---|---|
| 12.14 | Howland Street, Tottenham Court Road. Overhead wires down, debris on roadway, trolleybuses turning short at Cobden Statue, Mornington Crescent. | Four motor buses also damaged (including RT.66 "blasted to bits". |
| 12.27 | Esher - Ewell Road and Rushill Road, Long Ditton. 2 buses on Route 602, windows blasted. | |

| 171. | F.2490 | Tottenham Court Road Terminus | 10.12.36 | Clockwise via Howland Street, Fitzroy Street or Whitfield St. and Maple St. |
|---|---|---|---|---|

Edmonton's 1191 moves from
Fitzroy Street into Maple
Street on the 627; its next trip
is to Ponders End. Years later
a smart-looking 1143 also on
route 627 performs the same
manoeuvre. In the intervening
years the proprietors of the
building on the right have
moved. Before 1143 reached
Tottenham Court Road an
inspector observed it was
running late and instructed
its crew to curtail at SNELLS
PARK TOTTENHAM rather
than proceed to Edmonton
Town Hall. 1143 was one of
twenty-nine K1s sent from
Wood Green to Isleworth
depot at stage ten of the
conversion scheme. 1143's
conductor strolls across the
road – why! *John L. Smith/*
*Fred Ivey*

Very unusual is to see AEC J
912 working out of Leyland
depot Wood Green – WN
must be short of vehicles and
have called on Finchley to
help out. 912, a 629 to Enfield
turns from Fitzroy Street into
Maple Street sometime in the
mid-1950s. *Alan Cross*

At the very top of Maple Street there was a single bracket arm; four vehicles are parked adjacent to it. The leading vehicle is 1354 (the highest numbered K2) which is on route 629. Note the advertisements on the bombsite wall; 1354 promotes Sun Valley tobacco on the front and Nelson tipped cigarettes on the side.

*Bob Mack*

A trolley-jam! It would have been much better if 1053's driver had moved further down Maple Street; this would have allowed the trolleybuses behind to be parked more professionally - the sixth vehicle is blocking the Fitzroy Street/Maple Street junction. 1053 has a long trip ahead of it on the 627 to Waltham Cross.

*Michael Dryhurst*

As the end of each traffic day approached there were a number of trolleybus services which did not travel the full length of the route – the 653 was one. After the last Aldgate had left Tottenham Court Road some went to Hackney Station after which a few went to Stamford Hill only, with 1369 being an example of this. In the other direction the last few journeys only went as far as Mornington Crescent; route 653 was the only service where the last journeys in each direction did not travel the full length of its route. 1369 is the sole vehicle in Maple Street as the day of 22nd January 1961 comes to an end. A 'Buses for Trolleybuses' poster is pasted onto a traction pole; 1369 advertises the Sunday Telegraph which will be first published on 5th February. L1 1369 will have been withdrawn five days by then.

*Denis Battams*

K3 1680 was the sole member of the class to retain a two piece grille from delivery in 1940 until the withdrawal of the last K3s in July 196... With so many other K1s/K2s receiving maintenance at Edmonton depot, it is no small wonder that there was a lot of 'mix and match' there. Seen at the Tottenham Court Road terminus, 1680 waits out time before heading for Waltham Cross on route 627.

*Alan Cross*

The P1 class comprised twenty-five vehicles; many were allocated to Edmonton depot. One was 1717 which is running in on the 627; the destination display on paper blinds for Edmonton depot was **EDMONTON TRAMWAY AVENUE**.

*John L. Smith*

There were ten L2s with 954 being delivered fourteen months before the main batch. It spent a short time at West Ham depot before going to Holloway where it spent most of its life. It could be seen on all of its services and on the day that 954 was caught on camera in Maple Street it was operating on route 653.

*Alan Cross*

Looking in the opposite direction, Edmonton's 1186 is third in line in Maple Street. The conductor has wound the destination blind up a bit too far as it shows **WALTHAM CROSS VIA FINSBURY PARK FARRINGDON RD**. Route 627 did not travel by Farringdon Road! Also seen from the rear is K1 1259 – a 629 to Enfield; unusually it does not carry a rear advert. Five vehicles are parked up on this occasion.
*Michael Dryhurst/*
*John Buckle*

An anomaly at Wood Green depot between June 1954 and February 1955 was the allocation of D2 433 which waits outside an area destroyed by bombing during the war. 433 is a Leyland and therefore compatible with Wood Green's stock; working on route 629 to Enfield was regular for this vehicle.
*John L. Smith*

It was necessary for trainees to experience as much of the wiring associated with the depot to which they were to be allocated as possible. Highgate's 1362 is being used in this capacity and is parked with its poles down in Maple Street; behind, 778 on route 629, is on full lock.

*S.N.J. White*

Maple Street was used to curtail late-running buses on various routes using Tottenham Court Road; in this instance RTW 17 on route 14. They are six inches wider than the more abundant RTs/RTL but P1 1712, just commencing its trip to **TOWN HALL EDMONTON** on route 627 has no trouble overtaking.

*Michael Dryhurst*

Although there was a passing loop at the bottom of Maple Street, if vehicles had to pass each other further up then trolley booms had to be dropped. In May 1960, K 1261 on the 629 overtakes L 1435 on the 653. Both had been re-allocated during the conversion programme; 1261 transferred from Clapton to Wood Green while 1435 moved from West Ham to Highgate.

Some F1s were sent to Highgate depot in 1955 – all in the 740/750 series. Arriving in the summer of 1958 however was 654, the lowest numbered member of the class; Highgate were the main contributor to route 627. F1 654 (and the trolleybus behind) advertise one of London Transport's gimmick slogans: **HOP ON A BUS – 'HOP ON A TROLLEYBUS'** was never placed on trolleybuses!
*Michael Dryhurst*

To kick-start the Wood Green tram to trolleybus conversion on time (8th May 1938) it was necessary to place some brand-new J2s into service there; these worked alongside the native H1s for a few weeks until more of this class were delivered. J2 975 is in Maple Street; it will soon be off to Enfield on the 629.

*Charles Klapper*

Some N2s came to Highgate depot in the mid-fifties; one was 1653 which will soon depart for Aldgate on the 653 - route number and registration numbers match. When 'Len' took this photo, he would have had no idea it would be the last London trolleybus to be broken up in Great Britain.
*John L. Smith*

Fred Reynolds had a penchant for taking rear views of non-standard trolleybuses; this is shown by various Highgate
vehicles. L2 954 and X5 1379 were allocated to the 627 on the day these shots were taken. 954 is going to Edmonton
Town Hall while 1379 is running into Highgate depot as there is no relieving crew at **NAGS HEAD HOLLOWAY**.
Apart from a central cream band below the front windscreen, 954 looked the same at the front and the back as
standard vehicles; the same could not be said about 1379 which had a straight rear end. 1379 has offside platform
doors; these were provided for possible use in the Kingsway tram subway. There was an unsuccessful experiment
run in the subway in August 1939; thereafter the doors remained permanently closed.

*Fred Reynolds*

A bit further down the street, Mr Reynolds photographs 'Father of the Fleet' X2 62. According to the running number in the front view, 62 is HT1 on route 627; the offside view indicates a different number so maybe Mr Reynolds had two visits to Maple Street. Alternatively, depot staff have got their running numbers mixed up (later Highgate 627s were given running numbers in the 190/200 series). Very noticeable is the fact that 62 does not have a rear registration number in the usual position; it is positioned on the platform bulkhead. *Fred Reynolds*

**Looking suave and smart are two of Wood Green's finest - H1 774 and H1A 792A which are operating on rout**
**629; neither carry front advertisements. Both were overhauled in the summer of 1953 so maybe adverts are ye**
**to be applied. In the background of the 774 view, many people queue for a 627 or a 653.**
*Fred Reynole*

KI 1149 working on route 627 is in Maple Street during the use of the emergency wires – 16th to 18th June 1960; a fire had necessitated this. For the duration this is where passengers boarded. KI 1149 had been the last standard trolleybus to be overhauled; it was released from Fulwell works on 1st December 1959 but did not re-enter service until 7th March 1960 when it was allocated to Edmonton depot; in this view it is running into EM. K2 1352 turns from Maple Street into Whitfield Street; its next trip is to Enfield on route 629.

*Michael Dryhurst*

The facing frog near the bottom of Maple Street is shown to full effect in this view on 7th January 1961; L3 1448 rests on the siding before setting off for Aldgate on the 653. The wires leading off to the right form part of the alternative set of wiring; for a short distance, there are three sets of parallel wires in this street.

*Jack Gready*

The siding was a useful facility and allowed trolleybuses to overtake one another when necessary; in this instance two Wood Green vehicles take up the offer. K1 1061, working to Edmonton Town Hall on the 627 overtakes K2 1351 which will soon depart for Enfield on route 629. The bus stop flag is for routes 253, 627 and 629.
*Don Lewis*

Roadworks are occurring at the lower end of Maple Street. Bearing in mind that this is one-way traffic at present what is 1543B, working on route 653, using the siding when the regular set of wires seems to be available? A NO-ENTRY sign prevents motorists from accessing Maple Street from the other direction.
*Don Thompson*

Another enthusiast with a penchant for rear ends was Don Lewis who photographed N1 1560 leaving Maple Street for Edmonton Town Hall on route 627. He has also captured on film the two trailing frogs, the facing frog and the crossover that were positioned here.    *Don Lewis*

The photographer was 'in the know' about the emergency arrangements at Tottenham Court Road in June 1960. This was a busy time for inspectors who had to ensure the regularity of trolleybus services and control the anti-clockwise turning arrangements but also to supervise temporary boarding arrangements. N1 1566 and L3 1439 on the 627 and 653 respectively (both already having had their front blinds changed) move into Maple Street from Tottenham Court Road under their supervision. It is thought that the frog handle that gave access to these wires was locked in the 'down' position for the duration (it is unlikely that London Transport would have allowed conductors to run into the roadway after their vehicles during busy times - as shown in these views - and in darkness).

*Michael Dryhurst*

K1 1270 is seen at the junction of Maple Street with Tottenham Court Road on 11th March 1961. There was a tendency for drivers on routes 627/629/653 to change their destination blind well before the terminus – a Wood Green driver in this instance. The crossover and trailing frog for the 'alternative set of wires' are shown to full effect; its facing frog can just about be made out.

*John Gillham*

E3 car 1948 moves pa
Highbury and Islingto
station on a route 33 'depe
working'. When it gets t
**AGRICULTURAL HALL** a
Islington the driver will chang
from one end of the tram to th
other in order to reverse. Th
will allow 1948 to head alon
Essex Road to Manor Hous
Going in the other direction i
what is believed to be J3 105
on route 611. The crossove
and the trailing frog seen in th
view are part of the origina
layout.

MESSAGE FROM CONTROLLER
(CENTRAL ROAD SERVICES)

A.H. GRAINGER ESQ.

To
Date 28.11.52.    Place    HIGHBURY CORNER.    Time received

Route No.    Garage    Time occurred

TROLLEYBUS DELAY.
Routes 609, 611, 679 delayed from 11.10 to 11.45 a.m., wires
down.   Single-line operation from 11.45 a.m., until 1.10 p.m.,
when normal working was resumed.   The roof and side of a bus
on Route 43 ex Muswell Hill garage was scorched by falling wire
the bus was sent to garage.

Bus Routes 4,4A,19,30 were diverted southbound via Compton Road
and Canonbury Lane from 11.20 to 11.40 a.m., due to congestion
caused by the above derailment.

The damage to the bus is slight, the scorching causing a small
hole in the roof and scorching covering about 18 inches.   There
is also slight scorching down the side panel.

No personal injuries.

O  E OF THE OPERATING MANAGER (CENTRAL ROAD SERVICES)
40z/r120 (3)
(90/150  10/51-D30)

The image is described as: **Highbury Corner, Holloway Road**
**Canonbury Road looking south east.** The subject of this view outside
Highbury and Islington station on 2nd July 1960 is the facing frog which
splits 611s going towards Moorgate from 609s/679s heading toward
Islington.
*John Gillham*

E3 182 is by Islington Centra
Library at Fieldway Crescen
in Holloway Road travellin
south on route 35 to **NEW**
**X & FOREST HILL** on 10t
February 1952; the 'odd
blind display was one o
the idiosyncrasies that wa
typical of Charlton Work'
staff. Tram route 35 worke
between Forest Hill an
Highgate, a long way from
home for New Cross crew
similarly, it was a long wa
from base for Highgate sta
arriving at Forest Hill.
*Peter Mitchell 314*

# TIMES OF FIRST AND LAST TROLLEYBUSES

## Route 609
### BARNET AND MOORGATE

## Route 611
### HIGHGATE VILLAGE AND MOORGATE

## Route 679
### WALTHAM CROSS AND SMITHFIELD
AND CONNECTIONS

| FROM | TO | MONDAY to FRIDAY | | SATURDAYS | | SUNDAYS | |
|---|---|---|---|---|---|---|---|
| | | First | Last | First | Last | First | Last |
| | | Morning | Night | Morning | Night | Morning | Night |
| Barnet Church | Moorgate ... ... | 5 39 | 11 39 | 5 39 | 11 32 | 9 13 | 11 36 |
| Ponders End (Southbury Rd.) | Smithfield ... ... | 6 1 | 10 43 | 6 1 | 11 5 | 8 42 | 10 47 |
| Waltham Cross | Smithfield ... ... | 6 31 | 10 32 | 6 31 | 10 52 | 8 30 | 10 35 |
| Highgate Village | Moorgate ... ... | 7 8 | 11 22 | 7 8 | 11 54 | 7 21 | 11 46 |
| | Highgate (Archway Tavern) | 7 8 | 12 0 | 7 8 | 12 34 | 7 21 | 12 26 |
| Holloway (Nags Head) | Barnet ... ... | 6 28 | 11 19 | 6 28 | 11 48 | 8 30 | 11 11 |
| | North Finchley ... ... | 5 49 | 12 55 | 5 49 | 12 54 | 7 54 | 12 7 |
| | Highgate ... ... | 5 49 | 12 55 | 5 49 | (1 10 / 2 0) | 6 54 | 12 55 |
| | Highgate Village | 7 7 | 11 44 | 7 7 | 12 19 | 8 12 | 12 11 |
| | Ponders End ... ... | 5 11 | 11 54 | 5 11 | 12 39 | 9 48 | 11 37 |
| | Waltham Cross... ... | 5 11 | 11 41 | 5 11 | 12 39 | 9 48 | 11 37 |
| | Moorgate ... ... | 5 6 | 12 16 | 5 6 | 12 11 | 6 14 | 12 14 |
| | Smithfield ... ... | (†3 28 / †3 58) | 11 20 | (†3 28 / †3 58) | 11 43 | 9 18 | 11 23 |
| Highbury Station | Barnet ... ... | 6 22 | 11 13 | 6 22 | 11 42 | 8 24 | 11 5 |
| | North Finchley ... ... | 5 43 | 12 49 | 5 43 | 12 48 | 7 48 | 12 1 |
| | Highgate ... ... | 5 43 | 12 49 | 5 43 | (1 4 / 1 54) | 6 48 | 12 49 |
| | Highgate Village | 7 1 | 11 38 | 7 1 | 12 13 | 8 6 | 12 5 |
| | Ponders End ... ... | 5 59 | 11 49 | 5 59 | 12 16 | 9 48 | 11 28 |
| | Waltham Cross... ... | 5 59 | 10 36 | 5 59 | 10 48 | 9 48 | 11 28 |
| | Moorgate ... ... | 5 12 | 12 22 | 5 12 | 12 17 | 6 20 | 12 20 |
| | Smithfield ... ... | 3.33, 4.3 | 11 25 | 3.33, 4.3 | 11 49 | 9 23 | 11 28 |
| Moorgate | Barnet ... ... | 6 9 | 11 0 | 6 9 | 11 29 | 8 11 | 10 52 |
| | North Finchley ... ... | 5 30 | 12 36 | 5 30 | 12 35 | 7 35 | 11 48 |
| | Highgate ... ... | 5 30 | 12 36 | 5 30 | 12 35 | 6 35 | 12 36 |
| | Highgate Village | 6 51 | 11 27 | 6 51 | 12 2 | 7 55 | 11 54 |
| Smithfield | Ponders End ... ... | 5 48 | 11 38 | 5 48 | 12 5 | 9 37 | 11 17 |
| | Waltham Cross... ... | 5 48 | 10 25 | 5 48 | 10 37 | 9 37 | 11 17 |

† From Highgate 8 minutes earlier

### SERVICE INTERVALS.

| BETWEEN | MON. to FRI. | | SATURDAY | | SUNDAY | |
|---|---|---|---|---|---|---|
| | Peak | Normal | Peak | Normal | Morn. | Aftn. |
| | mins. | mins. | mins. | mins. | mins. | mins. |
| Barnet and Moorgate ... ... ... ... | 6 | 8 | 6 | 6 | 8 | 8 |
| Barnet and Islington Green ... ... ... | 6 | 8 | 6 | 6 | 8 | 4 |
| Highgate Village and Moorgate ... ... | 4 | 6 | 4 | 6 | 5 | 8 |
| Waltham Cross and Smithfield ... ... ... | 6 | 8 | 6 | 6 | 10 | 8 |

ON PUBLIC HOLIDAYS trolleybuses run at special times which are advertised on the vehicles

ALL ENQUIRIES TO LONDON TRANSPORT, 55 BROADWAY, S.W.I. ABBey 1234. 70

For posting between Holloway (Nags Head) and Highbury Station.

39—1955D—Proof

Waterlow & Sons Limited, London & Dunstable.

E3 car 185 is by Liverpool Road in Holloway Road working on route 35 on Sunday 10th February 1952; just discernible through the mist are the Holloway Road bridges. It is 11.58am and there is a surprising lack of motor and pedestrian traffic – maybe everyone is in church! 185 has been a Holloway depot for many years; upon its re-naming in July 1950, it became a Highgate depot car.

*Peter Mitchell 314*

There were two main thoroughfares served by London trolleybuses that had no places of great interest between Harlesden College Park and Paddington on the 662/664 and from Nags Head to Highbury Corner on routes 609/611/679. Illustrating the latter at George's Road in Holloway Road on 7th May 1961, L3 1520 heads for Moorgate on the 609.

*Peter Mitchell 1722*

E3 184 is beneath the southernmost bridge in Holloway Road on 10th February 1952 but only going to Kennington on route 33. Passengers could travel from Pemberton Gardens (where 184s journey started) to West Norwood on these depot workings, classified as 'when working' in London Transport parlance. In the background a trolleybus lurks beneath the bridge on which a large advertisement for MILITARY Pickle can be seen. *Peter Mitchell 3142*

..1 1369 working on route 611 to Moorgate is parked at the southbound bus stop just beyond the Holloway Road ..ridges which are used by British Railways trains that do not stop here. To the left is the entrance to Holloway ..oad underground station where tube trains run beneath ground. It is Sunday 17th July 1960 so route 611 will only ..e seen here for another two days. The bus stop on the left is a request stop so it is safe to assume that its opposite ..umber is of that status too. The gimmicky **TYRESOLES** advert on the bridge is prominent.          *Denis Battams*

..oadworks preclude buses, trams and trolleybuses from setting down and picking up passengers at the stop ..efore Holloway Road bridges.  The combined bus/trolleybus/tram stop has a hood over it, indicating to would- ..e passengers that it is not in use.  There may be staff at each end of the obstruction with bamboo poles as it is ..nlikely that trolley booms on vehicles travelling north will stretch far enough without dewiring, and that there ..ould be some 'wrong road running'.  However, if northbound trolleybuses are allowed to use the northbound ..verhead they will be travelling at very low speed.  Despite the restrictions, E3 tram 1981 working on route 35 to ..orest Hill is picking up passengers one Sunday.  Assuming that trams still use the northbound track, drivers will ..e under instructions to travel at very low speed past the roadworks.          *Don Thompson*

With the Holloway Road bridge in the background L1 1360 on route 611 heads for Moorgate passing an L3 on route 609 to Barnet. The photographer has gained access to an upstairs window to obtain this shot.

*Prince Marshall courtesy Alan Cross*

An unidentified 679 has suffered a dramatic dewirement when its trolley arms took the wrong set of wires at the Camden Road/Holloway Road junction while on its way to Smithfield; it is not known if this was human or mechanical error. The nearside boom is badly bent and needs major attention by a breakdown crew. A dewirement at this location related by an Edmonton driver had a lucky outcome; his 67? had taken the offside wires rather than the nearside ones. Both booms bounced off the overhead, swung around and repositioned themselves back onto the correct set of wires. The compiler of this book saw a similar incident at City Road junction in Cardiff where the nearside trolley arm bounced off the overhead, swung around and repositioned itself back onto it with the crew knowing little about it.

*J.H.Price*

In Holloway Road and slightly east of Camden Road is 1449 the lowest numbered L3 at Finchley depot. It heads south to Moorgate on route 609 on 7th May 1961.

*Peter Mitchell 1721*

126

Former Leyton E3 184 (now London Transport 184) heads south on route 35 at 11.34am on remembrance Sunday 11th November 1951. The conductor has failed to change the destination blind from **HIGHGATE** to show its south London terminus which presumably is **Forest Hill**. 184 has just passed beneath the massive trolleybus overhead complex at Nags Head Holloway. Also seen is the rear of J3 1052 whose conductor has set its blinds with precision for its trip on route 611 to **HIGHGATE VILLAGE**. Both vehicles are allocated to Highgate depot.

*Peter Mitchell 2936*

It is 20th January 1952, which is a Sunday and explains the lack of traffic in this view at Nags Head, Holloway. Trolleybus 910 and an unidentified tram wait for the 'off' at the traffic lights. The trolleybus is heading for Moorgate on the 609, with the tram working on route 35 to Forest Hill; they will parallel each other to Angel Islington - who will get there first?

*Julian Thompson courtesy Online Transport Archive*

This wonderful view of 754 was taken opposite Tufnell Park Road (just before Nags Head Holloway) on Saturday 16th August 1952; this experimental vehicle was regularly seen on route 609. Its closed-off front exit is shown to full-effect. Opposite is the Gaumont cinema which was badly damaged during the war.

*Peter Grace*

1269 awaits passengers while having some stand time at Moorgate; soon it will set off for Winchmore Hill on the 641. K1 1269 moved around the depots over the years with Wood Green being its last.
*Tony Belton*

With a number of Finchley's C3s being fitted with rear wheel spats they could be seen at Moorgate on route 609 from time to time. Exemplifying this is 317 whose driver is having a chat with an inspector on the south side of Finsbury Square.
*London Transport Museum G1319*

M1 1552 is the first of four trolleybuses parked on the east side of Finsbury Square at Moorgate; it will soon depart for Hampstead Heath on route 639. Its paintwork is poor as is the 611 which is two vehicles behind it. These two vehicles' external condition is in stark contrast to the 641 sandwiched between them; Wood Green maintenance staff took pride in the way in which they presented vehicles for service. A bamboo pole is attached to the traction standard on the right, allowing easy access to an implement that allows one trolleybus to overtake another.

On a wet day, L3 1452 has just left Moorgate for a trip on route 609 to the Hertfordshire town of Barnet. Two bowstring bracket arms are used in Finsbury Pavement.

*Geoff Lumb*

> ## 32 Bamboo Trolley Poles
> **(Trolleybuses)**
> The consumption of bamboo trolley poles is steadily increasing due to damage or loss of these poles, and the cost of replacement at the present time is very high.
> Staff are reminded to exercise great care in the use of these poles, as damage is frequently caused by allowing them to fall to the ground. Also, in order to avoid loss, it is important to ensure that the pole, when pushed fully into the space provided on the vehicle, is held by the retaining clip in the retainer, and that when fitted, the spring cover is closed.

An example of a bamboo pole is shown in the image of 1269 on the opposite page.

The photographer worked in the inner area of London and took the opportunity to record on colour film trolleybuses in the vicinity of his workplace during his lunchbreak one day. L3 1410 moves into Finsbury Square with the driver having already changed the destination blind for its next trip - to Parliament Hill Fields on route 615. The 'backward twins' advertisements show up well as does the Ben Truman one on the side. Very prominent are 'fairy-lights' adjacent to the running wires; when illuminated they gave guidance to drivers as to where they should position their vehicles when entering Moorgate terminus in poor weather.

*Roy Hubble*

J2 1002 has just passed through the City Road/Old Street junction while working on route 615 to Parliament Hill Fields. The conductor is on the platform ready to pull the semi automatic frog handle down at the City Road/East Road junction. *Roy Hubble*

The mid-fifties service cuts saw some newer machines allocated to Highgate depot; this is illustrated by F1 750 and M1 1551 in Pancras Road at Kings Cross. 750 works on route 639 to Moorgate while 1551 is only going as far as Kings Cross on the 615. Both are fitted with linen blinds in their front boxes before long they will be replaced by 'paper' ones. *Jim Copland*

Having been operating in the east end of London since new, M1 1548 came to Highgate depot in April 1960; it is having a year's service at HT. When this image was taken at the Tottenham Court Road terminus it was working on route 627 to Waltham Cross.

These views were taken before metal depot code plates were replaced by painted ones – prior to April 1960. Showing this feature at Tottenham Court Road terminus are Edmonton's 1231 on route 627 and Highgate's 1045 on the 653. Remnants of bomb damage are seen in the picture of K2 1231 whose driver is not showing WALTHAM CROSS accurately; it has no offside advertisement though 'HOP ON A BUS' is displayed on its front. 1045's driver should move his vehicle up so that the trio behind can get in better positions further down Maple Street.

*Michael Dryhurst*

Another Highgate trolleybu seen at Maple Street terminu is K2 1317 which is on the insid track there. Highgate onl had a small number of K clas vehicles; 1317 resided there fo much of its life.

*London Transport Museum G132*

Finchley maintenance sta always kept their vehicles in very presentable condition wit this being well illustrated in th view of L3 1500 is in Grays In Road while working on rout 621 to Holborn Circus. Havin been impeded at a bus stop b a **WHITE HEATHER MODE LAUNDRY** van, 1500's drive puts his right hand out of th side cab window to indicat his intentions to other roa users. 1500 was one of Finchle depots' latter day trainin vehicles.

L3 1428 was allocated to rout 517 on the day this image wa taken; it works as HT89 in th service. At Holloway depot from new it remained at a re-name Highgate until stage nine of th conversion programme. 1428 i in Grays Inn Road and will soo reach Holborn Circus terminu **BRYMAY** safety matche ceased to be manufactured i 1960. *Roy Broo*

PI 1705, working the full length of the route 659 to Waltham Cross, leaves Charterhouse Street to enter Holborn; it passes Prince Albert's statue. With no pedestrians nor any other vehicle this photograph must have been taken on a Sunday. This colour view allows the **COPES** advertisements to be viewed to full effect.

*Don Thompson*

L3 1512 pauses in Charterhouse Street, having a rest from its labours on route 621. Trolleybuses will not be operating here much longer as a yellow sticker on the bus stop flag indicates the withdrawal of the last Holborn loop services in a few days' time. Additional information about the changeover is seen on a nearside window of 1512 and on a traction standard by the bus stop.     *Tony Belton*

JI 920 is nearing the end of its journey to Holborn Circus on route 621; the driver has prematurely changed the front destination blind to show **NORTH FINCHLEY**. The vehicle is in Farringdon Road with an arrow on a building pointing to Farringdon Station. 920 is very smart. The JIs were synonymous with Finchley depot.

*Marcus Eavis courtesy Online Transport Archive*

Kings Cross Road was a dreary place at the best of times but drearier when it rained. This is exemplified by N2 1653 which is working to North Finchley on route 517.          *Jim Copland*

Not far away from the previous photograph, L3 1421 is in Caledonian Road midway between Pentonville Road and Caledonia Street. It also is working on route 517 to North Finchley.          *Jim Copland*

Turning from Holloway Road into Camden Road on 23rd October 1961, L3 1487 is only going as far as Kings Cross on the 621. When it came to selecting the L3s to be forwarded from Finchley to Fulwell depot at conversion stage twelve, 1487 was not considered to be in good enough condition for further use. It was sold to Cohen's for scrap on 13th November – just six days earlier it had been carrying passengers in north London. See page 49.

*Peter Mitchell 19402*

It was common for 627s to be curtailed at Nags Head Holloway; to make the manoeuvre, they turned left from Seven Sisters Road into Holloway Road, right into Camden Road and right again to stand in Warlters Road. Edmonton's 1089 is running late so has been curtailed there; it will pick up its time in due course. The most likely explanation for Highgate's 1560 turning here is there is no relieving crew in Parkhurst Road to take it on to Tottenham Court Road so is temporarily taken out of service – maybe it will start its northbound timing in Parkhurst Road. Note the two different ways that NAGS HEAD HOLLOWAY is shown by two different depots.

*Peter Moore*

1336 on route 659 has been curtailed at **NAGS HEAD HOLLOWAY**.  It enters Warlters Road where it will have some stand time before picking up its correct order in the northbound service. The building to the left is Warlter sub-station.

*Tony Belto*

L3 1469 moves from Camden Road into Caledonian Road on 18th April 1960; it is heading for Holborn Circus on route 621. The single-track wires going off to the left lead into Warlters Road.

*Clarence Carte*

At the very top end of Caledonian Road and by Widdenham Road L3 1408 is on its way to Holborn Circus on route 517 on 24th September 1955. Caledonian Road was colloquially known as 'The Cally'.

*Peter Mitchell 8311*

K2 1164 was always allocated to Edmonton depot, so working on route 659 is typical. It is seen at Stock Orchard Street on 16th August 1958.

*Peter Mitchell 11698*

J1 916 crosses Caledonian Road over-bridge while working on route 521 to Holborn Circus on 13th April 1959; behind, K2 1170 also works to Holborn Circus but on the 659. An advertisement by the Finsbury Park Empire for forthcoming shows is on a billboard affixed on the bridge.

*John Clarke*

L3 1464 on the 52 passes Caledonian Road underground station on 31st August 1961. The destination blind is badly set as it shows **HOLBORN CIRCUS** in the middle of the blind rather than at the bottom. 1464 was the last trolleybus up and down Caledonian Road very late in the evening of 7th November 1961. *Peter Mitchell 1877*

K2 1175 is by Blundell Street while working on route 659 to Holborn Circus on 6th August 1960; on the right is a wall of Pentonville prison. Going the other way is RT 2042 which is heading for Hornsey Rise on route 14. *Peter Mitchell 157*

*The details of this photograph are incorporated in the caption on the following page.*

On Sunday 8th March 1959 (four days after the start of the trolleybus conversion scheme) London Transport and British Railways activated a well organised plan whereby a new bridge was rolled in across Caledonian Road; motor traffic was diverted but, with no alternative routeing, trolleybuses continued to use Caledonian Road. The power was cut off with trolleybuses heading north being towed for a number of yards; those heading south did so in battery mode, either with their poles on the wires or under their retaining hooks. The first view shows an unidentified northbound 621 having its trolley arms replaced on the overhead having been towed up the incline; the second shows a southbound 521 - NIA 1587A – with its lights on, its trolley booms down and a badly set destination blind. Going south in the other views: 1054's poles are on the overhead so the 517's driver passes through on a combination of battery and gravity power - this is also occurring to a 659 as its valance is still in position.

*Fred Ivey*

Another Finchley trolleybus with its destination blind badly set is L3 1478 which has just passed Offord Road on 7th February 1961. The display implies that it is heading for Finchley on the 521 when in fact it is going to Holborn Circus.     *Peter Mitchell 1671*

The next view Mr Mitchell took was of 1236 passing Story Street while working on the 659 to Holborn Circus on 7th February 1961. The front advert is for the Sunday Telegraph which had been initially published two days earlier.     *Peter Mitchell 1672*

914 is by Twyford Street on 14th September 1955, working as a 621 to Holborn Circus. It was one of three J1s sent from Finchley to Highgate at stage four of the conversion scheme; it stayed just until stage five when withdrawal occurred. Therefore, it operated in Caledonian Road on the 521/621 for 28 years and then on the 517/617 for twelve weeks. It is unlikely that any passenger was aware of this     *Peter Mitchell 831*

**n 1st September 1961 L3 1507 is by Carnegie Street which is south of Copenhagen Street; this was fare stage six n all trolleybus routes using Caledonian Road. 1507 heads for Holborn Circus on route 521; behind is the enemy, a notorbus on route 17 which replaced trolleybus routes 517/617 exactly seven months earlier. 1507 was withdrawn t stage twelve of the conversion scheme – 8th November 1961. Intriguingly, it was reinstated to Stonebridge two eeks later – 22nd November. It did not stay in service until the end at SE - 2nd January 1962 - but managed to nake its own way to Colindale depot for storage that evening.** *Peter Mitchell 18784*

FARES

ROUTE 521—HOLBORN & NORTH FINCHLEY (F.T.2176) (Aug. 1956)

Via Grays Inn Road

ROUTE 621—HOLBORN & NORTH FINCHLEY

Via Farringdon Road

| Stage Point No. | | | | | | | | | | | | | | | | | | | | | | |
|---|---|---|---|---|---|---|---|---|---|---|---|---|---|---|---|---|---|---|---|---|---|---|
| 3 | Holborn, Grays Inn Road, Holborn Circus or Farringdon Station–3 | | | | | | | | | | | | | | | | | | | | | |
| 4 | 2½ | Guilford Street (Short Route )(521) or Rosebery Avenue, Farringdon Road (Short Route) (621)–4 | | | | | | | | | | | | | | | | | | | | |
| 5 | 2½ | 2½ | Kings Cross Stations–5† | | | | | | | | | | | | | | | | | | | |
| 6 | 4 | 2½ | 2½ | Copenhagen Street–6✱ | | | | | | | | | | | | | | | | | | |
| 7 | 4 | 4 | 2½ | 2½ | Offord Road–7 | | | | | | | | | | | | | | | | | |
| 8 | 6 | 4 | 4 | 2½ | 2½ | North Road–8 | | | | | | | | | | | | | | | | |
| 9 | 6 | 6 | 4 | 4 | 2½ | 2½ | Holloway Road, Nags Head–9 | | | | | | | | | | | | | | | |
| 10 | 8 | 6 | 6 | 4 | 4 | 2½ | 2½ | Hornsey Road–10✱ | | | | | | | | | | | | | | |
| 11 | 8 | 6 | 6 | 4 | 4 | 2½ | 2½ | 2½ | Finsbury Park Station–11 | | | | | | | | | | | | | |
| 12 | 8 | 8 | 6 | 6 | 4 | 4 | 2½ | 2½ | 2½ | Alexandra Grove (Pitmans College)–12✱ | | | | | | | | | | | | |
| 13 | 8 | 8 | 6 | 6 | 4 | 4 | 4 | 2½ | 2½ | 2½ | Manor House, Station–13 | | | | | | | | | | | |
| 14 | 10 | 8 | 8 | 6 | 6 | 4 | 4 | 4 | 2½ | 2½ | 2½ | Harringay Arena–14✱ | | | | | | | | | | |
| 15 | 10 | 10 | 8 | 8 | 6 | 6 | 4 | 4 | 4 | 2½ | 2½ | 2½ | Harringay, Salisbury Hotel–15 | | | | | | | | | |
| 16 | 1/- | 10 | 10 | 8 | 8 | 6 | 6 | 6 | 4 | 4 | 4 | 2½ | 2½ | Turnpike Lane Station–16 | | | | | | | | |
| 17 | 1/- | 1/- | 10 | 10 | 8 | 8 | 6 | 6 | 6 | 4 | 4 | 4 | 2½ | 2½ | Wood Green L.T. Station–17 | | | | | | | |
| 18 | 1/2 | 1/- | 1/- | 10 | 10 | 8 | 8 | 8 | 6 | 6 | 6 | 4 | 4 | 2½ | 2½ | Nightingale Road, Bounds Green Road–18 | | | | | | |
| 19 | 1/2 | 1/2 | 1/- | 1/- | 10 | 10 | 8 | 8 | 8 | 6 | 6 | 6 | 4 | 4 | 2½ | 2½ | Bounds Green Station or The Ranelagh–19 | | | | | |
| 20 | 1/4 | 1/2 | 1/2 | 1/- | 1/- | 10 | 10 | 10 | 8 | 8 | 8 | 6 | 6 | 4 | 4 | 2½ | 2½ | Palmers ~~Green~~–20 ROAD | | | | |
| 21 | 1/4 | 1/4 | 1/2 | 1/2 | 1/- | 1/- | 10 | 10 | 10 | 8 | 8 | 8 | 6 | 6 | 4 | 4 | 2½ | 2½ | New Southgate Station or Friern Hospital Gates–21 | | | |
| 22 | 1/5 | 1/4 | 1/4 | 1/2 | 1/2 | 1/- | 1/- | 1/- | 10 | 10 | 10 | 8 | 8 | 6 | 6 | 4 | 4 | 2½ | 2½ | Friern Barnet, Orange Tree–22 | | |
| 23 | 1/5 | 1/5 | 1/4 | 1/4 | 1/2 | 1/2 | 1/- | 1/- | 1/- | 10 | 10 | 10 | 8 | 8 | 6 | 6 | 4 | 4 | 2½ | 2½ | Hilton Avenue–23 | |
| 24 | 1/6 | 1/5 | 1/5 | 1/4 | 1/4 | 1/2 | 1/2 | 1/2 | 1/- | 1/- | 1/- | 10 | 10 | 8 | 8 | 6 | 6 | 4 | 4 | 2½ | 2½ | North Finchley, Tally Ho–24 |

✱ NEW FARE STAGES

6–Copenhagen Street
10–Hornsey Road
12–Alexandra Grove (Pitmans College)
14–Harringay Arena

†–Farezone

EARLY MORNING SINGLE FARES

| Where the Ordinary Single fare is | Early Morning Single fare will be |
|---|---|
| 8d. – 1/4 | 7d. |
| 1/5 – 1/6 | 8d. |

L3 1452 has just crossed Regents Canal bridge on Saturday 28th October 1961 - a glorious sunny day fo[r] photographing London trolleybuses; it heads for Holborn Circus on the 621. In London Transport's records 145[2] (along with 1449 and 1489) was forwarded from Poplar to Finchley depot on 12th January 1959 – however, [it] probably happened on 7th January, the day many service cuts were implemented. They were the forerunners o[f] what FY would get over the next year or so. *Peter Mitchell 1941[?]*

| F.2918 | Caledonian Rd., Canal Bdge. | 26. 5.38 | Clockwise circle of the triangle at junction of Caledonian Road and Southampton Street. | Battery emergency only. |
|---|---|---|---|---|

L3 1493 is passing All Saints Street in Caledonian Road while working on route 621 to Holborn Circus on 18th Ju[ly] 1961. There is a downhill slope in Caledonian Road before it reaches Pentonville Road. *Peter Mitchell 1834*

A few yards further south 1179 on the 659 is just a few minutes away from its destination of Holborn Circus; this vehicle was one of many K2s that stayed loyal to Edmonton depot throughout their lives. The shop adjacent to 1179 is a 'ladies only' establishment – only the bravest of men would make purchases there!

*Don Jones*

As already stated, Saturday 28th October 1961 was a sunny day and is confirmed by this view of L3 1461 on the 621 at the junction of Caledonian Road with Pentonville Road at Kings Cross. Behind, RTW 34 operates on bus route 14. Trolleybuses (and trams before them) were unable to make the sharp left turn from Caledonian Road into Pentonville Road so had to move into Grays Inn Road, then into Swinton Street and Farringdon Road to get to Holborn Circus.

*Peter Mitchell 19414*

## Christmas Day service for route 521/621
The 521 journey to Turnpike Lane was the only scheduled one of the year

62

### Routes 521-621. NORTH FINCHLEY - HOLBORN via Grays Inn Road & via Farringdon Road

Service interval : 16-20 minutes morning ; 10 minutes afternoon on each route.

|  | First |  |  |  |  |  |  |  |  | Last |  |  |  |  |  |  |  |  |  |  |  |  |  |  |  |
|---|---|---|---|---|---|---|---|---|---|---|---|---|---|---|---|---|---|---|---|---|---|---|---|---|---|
| NORTH FINCHLEY *Tally Ho* | 3 47 | .... | 5 35 | 6 7 | 6 41 | 7 4 | 7 24 | 7 43 | .... | 2 1 | 2 5 | 2 10 | 2 15 | 2 20 | 2 25 | 2 30 | 2 35 | 2 40 | 2 45 | 2 50 | 2 55 | 3 0 | 3 5 | 3 10 | .... |
| Wood Green *LT Station* | 4 5 | *5 13 | 5 53 | 6 25 | 6 59 | 7 22 | 7 42 | 8 1 | .. | 2 19 | 2 23 | 2 28 | 2 33 | 2 38 | 2 43 | 2 48 | 2 53 | 2 58 | 3 3 | 3 10 | 3 15 | 3 20 | 3 25 | 3 30 | .. |
| Finsbury Park *LT Station* | 4 18 | 5 24 | 6 6 | 6 38 | 7 12 | 7 35 | 7 55 | 8 14 | .... | 2 32 | 2 36 | 2 41 | 2 46 | 2 53 | 2 58 | 3 3 | 3 8 | 3 13 | 3 18 | .... | .... | .... | .... | .... | .. |
| King's Cross Station | 4 32 | 5 38 | 6 20 | 6 52 | 7 26 | 7 49 | 8 9 | 8 28 | .... | 2 46 | 2 50 | †2 57 | †3 2 | .... | .... | .... | .... | .... | .... | .... | .... | .... | .... | .... | .. |
| Holborn via *Grays Inn Road* | 4 39 | 5 45 | 6 27 | 6 59 | 7 33 | .... | 8 16 | .... | .... | 2 53 | .... | .... | .... | .... | .... | .... | .... | .... | .... | .... | .... | .... | .... | .... | .. |
| HOLBORN via *Farringdon Road* | .. | .. | .. | .. | .. | 7 56 | .. | 8 35 | .... | .. | 2 58 | .. | .. | .. | .. | .. | .. | .. | .. | .. | .. | .. | .. | .. | .. |
| | | | | | | | | | | | | | | | | | | | | | | | | | |
| HOLBORN CIRCUS | 4 39 | 5 45 | 6 27 | 6 59 | 7 33 | 7 56 | 8 16 | 8 35 | .... | 2 43 | .... | .... | 2 49 | .... | .... | 2 53 | .... | .... | 2 58 | .... | .... | ••• | ••• | .... | .. |
| Kings Cross via *Farringdon Road* | 4 46 | 5 52 | 6 34 | 7 6 | 7 40 | .... | 8 23 | .... | .... | 2 51 | .... | .... | .... | .... | .... | 3 1 | .... | .... | †3 0 | .... | .... | †3 5 | .... | .... | .. |
| Kings Cross via *Grays Inn Road* | .. | .. | .. | .. | .. | 8 3 | .. | 8 42 | .... | .. | .... | 2 56 | .... | .... | .... | .... | .... | 3 5 | .... | .... | 3 5 | .... | .... | .... | .. |
| Finsbury Park *LT Station* | 5 0 | 6 6 | 6 48 | 7 20 | 7 54 | 8 17 | 8 37 | 8 56 | .... | 3 5 | 3 5 | .... | 3 10 | 3 10 | .... | 3 15 | .... | 3 16 | 3 15 | 3 19 | .... | 3 21 | 3 20 | .... | .. |
| Wood Green *LT Station* | *5 11 | 6 19 | 7 1 | 7 33 | 8 7 | 8 30 | 8 50 | 9 9 | .. | 3 18 | 3 20 | 3 22 | 3 23 | 3 25 | 3 27 | 3 28 | .... | 3 29 | 3 30 | 3 32 | 3 33 | 3 34 | 3 35 | .... | .. |
| NORTH FINCHLEY *Tally Ho* | .. | 6 37 | 7 19 | 7 51 | 8 25 | 8 48 | 9 8 | 9 27 | .. | 3 36 | 3 38 | 3 40 | 3 41 | 3 43 | 3 45 | 3 46 | .... | 3 47 | 3 48 | 3 50 | 3 51 | 3 52 | 3 53 | .. | .. |

*–Time at Turnpike Lane *LT Station.*     †–Time at Swinton Street.

145

These views see trolleybuses moving out of Caledonian Road and crossing Pentonville Road to access Grays Inn Road. 1177 on the 659 is seen on 18th April 1960 with Highgate's 1061 on the 517 another time.    *Clarence Carter*
*Don Thompson*

Until 30th June 1933 tram route 21 was jointly operated by the Metropolitan Electric Tramways and London County Council; the following day both organisations became part of the London Transport empire. Ex-MET car 2264 appears to be held for its timing by an inspector at Kings Cross Bridge while working to Holborn. In the background, Premier Shoe Repairs charge 2/6d for ladies and 3/6d for men. It can just be made out that trolleybus overhead is in-situ – trams, take note!

Many years later 1408 on the 617 to Holborn Circus leads 1507 a 621 to Kings Cross over Kings Cross Bridge. The name for this thoroughfare can be seen on the building on the right.    *Tony Belton*

# 1732.—TROLLEYBUS CONVERSION—HOLLOWAY AND FINCHLEY DEPOTS AND OTHER ROUTE ALTERATIONS.

Notice to Inspectors and Conductors—Edmonton, Finchley, Hackney, Hampstead, Hendon, Holloway, Poplar, Stamford Hill, Stonebridge, Wood Green, Camberwell and Norwood Depots.

Commencing on Sunday, 6th March, 1938, the following route alterations will become effective :—

## 1. Conversions to Trolleybus operation.

| Existing Tram Route | New Trolleybus Route | | Remarks |
|---|---|---|---|
| | Number | Between | |
| 17 | 517/617 (Holloway Depot) | North Finchley Terminus and Holborn/ Farringdon Street Loop via Highgate | Routes running to London via Grays Inn Road will show 517 or 521 and will retain these numbers back to the Suburban Terminus. Routes to London via Farringdon Road will show 617 or 621 and retain these numbers back to the Suburban Terminus. |
| 21 | 521/621 (Finchley Depot) | North Finchley Terminus and Holborn/ Farringdon Street Loop via Finsbury Park | |
| 9 | 609 (Holloway Depot) | Barnet and Moorgate, Finsbury Square via Highgate | |

This view at Kings Cross Bridge was taken just before the start of services around the Holborn loop. A pair of Holloway's H1s are giving dignitaries an opportunity to travel on a new mode of transport in the area. Of the two trolleybuses, only 796 can be identified; it worked at Holloway, Bexleyheath and Walthamstow depots during its working life. It was withdrawn at stage four of the conversion scheme; London Transport then donated it to the Paris Transport Museum.
*Stilltime collection*

At Kings Cross Bridge on 11th December 1952, Edmonton's 1281 works on route 659. The driver has been 'slapdash' when turning the destination blind as it does not show the via point of FINSBURY PK for Waltham Cross. The policeman on point duty has distinctive white armbands.
*London Transport Museum U2320*

t Pancras Station is a famous London landmark and the background to 1409 which moves from Pancras Road into Euston Road on 17th December 1960; L3 1409 operates on route 613, heading for Holborn Circus. It is allocated to Highgate depot and has been there from new. A transfer to Fulwell will occur on the night of 31st January 1961; its oor condition will see it withdrawn nine months later. 1409 will be seen at another famous landmark - Hampton Court - during its time spent in West London.

*Ron Wellings*

**137 Resiting of Frog—Euston Road, Kings Cross**

(Trolleybus Routes 513, 613, 639)
Staff are notified that on and from Sunday, 29th July, the frog situate in Euston Road, Kings Cross, at the junction with York Way and Grays Inn Road, is to be resited from T.S. 45 to T.S. 46.

astbound 513s/613s and eastbound 615s/639s parted company outside Kings Cross station. On 31st December 960 L3 1382 moves onto the inner set of wires on its trip to Moorgate on the 615; an inspector pulls the frog andle down. The sign with an arrow directs people as to where trolleybuses can be boarded; a bamboo pole hangs n a traction standard.

*Jack Gready*

J2 986 has just passed King[']
Cross station and about t[o]
branch off into Grays In[n]
Road. It is working on rout[e]
513 to Holborn Circus in th[e]
summer of 1959. This vehic[le]
worked most of its life a[t]
Holloway/Highgate depo[t]
*Don Thompso[n]*

B3 487 is only going t[o]
**WINDSOR TERRACE CIT[Y]
ROAD** on route 639. Ove[r]
the whole trolleybus networ[k]
there were just two panel[s]
(both at Holloway) that use[d]
three lines to describe th[e]
destination on the blind; i[n]
this instance there are fou[r]
words also. 487 is passin[g]
Kings Cross Station.
*Geoff Baddele[y]*

Going south, one of Highgate['s]
original L3s - 1415 - is th[e]
victim of an unusual inciden[t]
The booms have split at th[e]
facing frog a few yards back[;]
the positive boom has followe[d]
the Grays Inn Road wirin[g]
with the negative boom takin[g]
the Pentonville Road wire[.]
Fortunately, the crew becam[e]
aware of the predicamen[t]
and resolved it with the ai[d]
of a trusty bamboo pole. 141[5]
moves from Euston Road int[o]
Grays Inn Road; it operates o[n]
route 513 to Holborn Circu[s]
Large metal signs prominentl[y]
point potential passengers t[o]
Kings Cross St Pancras an[d]
Euston stations. *Tony Belto[n]*

150

N1 1587 was an early wartime casualty at Bow depot; rebodied by Weymann's it was returned to London Transport as N1A 1587A. It was allocated to Fulwell depot initially but was transferred to Holloway in 1948. Seen at Kings Cross and just entering Grays Inn Road, it is operating on route 613 to Holborn Circus.          *Fred Ivey*

A few yards further on L3 1527, working only as far as Kings Cross on the 639, is at the junction of Kings Cross Bridge with Grays Inn Road. As in the view of 1415 on the previous page, 1527 has its route blind turned up a little bit too far; when route numbers did not align in their box, it was usually because the blind had slipped.          *Tony Belton*

On 31st January 1961 L3 1439 turns into Euston Road from Grays Inn Road at Kings Cross while working on route 613 to Hampstead Heath. On the left RTL 1426 has its offside rear trafficator blinking; it operates on route 18B to London Bridge. The 'Palladium' features Norman Wisdom in 'Turn Again Whittington'.          *Brian Speller*

Having left Holborn Circu[s] and travelled the length o[f] Grays Inn Road, J3 1047 is o[n] a section of overhead use[d] solely by 613s. Working t[o] Hampstead Heath it is abou[t] to enter Euston Road.

*Don Jone[s]*

D3 544 has had a trolley mishap at the Grays Inn Road[/] Kings Cross Bridge overhea[d] junction - maybe the pole[s] have taken the wires toward[s] Caledonian Road rathe[r] than those to Pancras Road[.] A member of staff is sortin[g] things out; 544 will the[n] progress on its journey t[o] Hampstead Heath on the 613[.]

*Fred Ive[y]*

These two photographs were taken on 31st December 1960 near the small thoroughfare of Kings Cross Bridge[.] Grays Inn Road is viewed from the north and the south with the three items of 'special work' erected here see[n] in both images. Stage nine of the conversion programme saw all 'special work' concerning the Hampstead route[s] having to be removed at Kings Cross. This was an enormous amount of work and would have been carried ou[t] over a few nights and probably with two gangs of linesmen, All that was left after this was just a crossover an[d] trailing frog that connected Pentonville Road with Caledonian Road.

*John Gillha[m]*

152

These excellent views taken in Grays Inn Road between Kings Cross Bridge and Swinton Street illustrate two Highgate vehicles working to Holborn Circus: 1549 on route 617 and 1370 on the 513. M1 1549 had worked at Bow and West Ham before coming to Highgate; 1370 had always been at Holloway/Highgate. 1370's destination blind sits well in its box – the same cannot be said for 1549 as it is fitted with a reduced depth blind with the destination box glass un-masked.

*Roy Vincent*

The facing frog that split trolleybuses going around the Holborn loop is illustrated in this view taken on 31st December 1960. An unidentified 617 has just moved onto the wiring that enables trolleybuses to turn left from Grays Inn Road into Swinton Street. K1 1066 has moved onto the same set of wires while operating a Kings Cross shortworking on route 615. *John Gillham/ Don Thompson*

L3 1424 on route 617 has its front wheels in Swinton Street on 31st December 1960. The destination blind shows it is running directly into Highgate depot; the most likely explanation is that 1424 does not have a relief crew at Highgate, Archway and the crew has been told by an official to run it directly into Highgate depot so as to avoid having 1424 being parked up in Archway Road. The driver has unnecessarily put the side-lights on; this means the saloon lights are also on. *Jack Gready*

Sunday 5th November 1961 and the **PSV** Circle have organised a tour around some of the remnants of the London trolleybus system on Wood Green's 1353. Aware that it would pass through Wood Green to get to the official starting point at Swinton Street at Kings Cross for a 10am start, some of the participants 'arranged' to board in Wood Green High Road. When K2 1353 passed through Kings Cross it was the only time this occurred during its lifetime. Finchley's 1548 on route 621 passes by.

*Dave Pearson*

Saturday 7th January 1961. Apart from Bank Holiday Mondays, route 639 did not have any scheduled workings that only went as far as Kings Cross; therefore, L3 1399 has been curtailed. Being a dull day, the driver has switched 1399s lights to the 'on' position; it stands on the siding at the bottom of Swinton Street. The 'Sunday Telegraph' was launched on 5th February 1961 so London Transport and the Sunday Telegraph owners are working well in advance of its publication date.

*Hugh Taylor*

At Swinton Street terminus on 3rd August 1959, two trolleybuses are parked on the siding; only 1355 on the 517 is identifiable. About to pass through the facing frog is Edmonton's 1193 on route 659.

*Mike Abbott*

No details wer‹ given on thes‹ instructions abou‹ the Holborn Circu‹ terminal; this wa‹ due to Holbor‹ having a no standin‹ time restriction.

From mid-afternoon until the end of traffic on Saturday‹ route 621 went no further than KINGS CROSS; therefor‹ 1488 has terminated in Swinton Street. The compiler of thi‹ book is pulling the frog handle down so that 1488 can acces‹ Kings Cross Road. The conductor is on the platform ensurin‹ safe operation through the facing frog. *Peter Moor‹*

L1 1367 has terminate‹ at the lower end o‹ Swinton Street on 11t‹ December 1960. It turn‹ left into Kings Cros‹ Road to pick up the 517' line of route; a 615 wil‹ soon enter the 'shunt' Passengers were allowe‹ to board trolleybuse‹ here. *Lyndon Row‹*

At the lower en‹ of Swinton Stree‹ overhead wiring allowe‹ trolleybuses to turn righ‹ and left. L3 1473, a 62‹ to North Finchley, ha‹ terminated in Swinto‹ Street; it now turns lef‹ into Kings Cross Road Alongside and turnin‹ right into Kings Cros‹ Road is L1 1357 on th‹ 613 to Holborn Circu‹ This intriguing pictur‹ taken on 23rd Decembe‹ 1959 shows routes i‹ the 600 series about t‹ travel clockwise and anti clockwise along King‹ Cross Road. *John Clark‹*

On 26th August 1956 J1 906 on the 521 is at the Grays Inn Road/Clerkenwell Road junction when the wiring layout was complete. On 31st December 1960 L3 1393 on route 517 makes the same manoeuvre through the reduced amount of overhead following the withdrawal of route 665 in November 1959.
*Don Thompson/ Jack Gready*

The driver of 1002 has paused at the traffic lights at the junction of Grays Inn Road with Clerkenwell Road to allow an unidentified 643 to get on its way to Wood Green on 31st October 1959. J2 1002 heads for Holborn Circus on route 513. *John Clarke*

The very noticeable 954 head for North Finchley on the 62 - it passes Theobalds Roa while moving north alon Grays Inn Road; alongside RTL 879 working on route 17 Westbound overhead see in the top of this view head towards Bloomsbury.

*Fred Ive*

Routes 555/581/665 have bee withdrawn, along with thei associated wiring, makin movements easier for driver turning from Grays Inn Roa into Clerkenwell Road a shown by K2 1205 on the 64 on 13th July 1961. Making th move in the other directio on the same date, and with Holborn Hall on its right, is K 1221 on route 543.

*Denis Battam*

Something was wrong with the Grays Inn Road/Clerkenwell Road semi-electric frog on 21st January 1961 with trolleybus after trolleybus dewiring; the photographer was informed of this by a bystander. In this instance K2 1177 on the 659 is the victim; overhead staff will soon arrive and rectify the matter. *Hugh Taylor*

| 521/ 621 | North Finchley, 'Tally Ho' (clockwise) |
|---|---|
| | *Friern Barnet, Summers Lane (clockwise) battery |
| | New Southgate, Station Road (clockwise) |
| | Wood Green Station (clockwise) |
| | Turnpike Lane Station (anti-clockwise) from south only |
| | †Manor House Station (clockwise) |
| | Finsbury Park, Coleridge Road (anti-clockwise) |
| | Holloway, Warlters Road (clockwise) before 7.30 a.m.: after 7.0 p.m. and * |
| | *Caledonian Road, Canal Bridge (clockwise) battery |
| | Kings Cross, Swinton Street (anti-clockwise) |
| | Clerkenwell Green (clockwise) |

No details were given on these instructions about the Holborn Circus terminal; this was due to Holborn having a no standing time restriction. 521s/621s cannot turn at Manor House station.

3 1511 on route 621 has just passed the facing frog at the junction of Grays Inn Road and Clerkenwell Road on 5th July 1961, three days before conversion stage eleven. Since 1939, conductors on routes heading for Kings Cross pulled the semi-automatic frog handle here - and this was despite the less frequent use of the right-hand turn into Clerkenwell Road by 643s. *John Gillham*

# LONDON operates nearly 2,000
## B.U.T. trolleybuses

*but they still* WANT MORE!

The vast trolleybus fleet serving London comes from the B.U.T. factories. It started that way, and has gone on like that ever since. Orders are in hand for more B.U.T.s, to satisfy the transport needs of the city's teeming millions. Many big cities in all 5 continents also rely on B.U.T. transport, because they cut running and maintenance costs and do a fine job of work in any sort of climate or route. There are 2- and 3-axle models; details upon application.

**BRITISH UNITED TRACTION LTD.**
HANOVER HOUSE · HANOVER SQUARE · LONDON, W.1

# *Busy Urban Transport*...

sets a problem that is best solved by B.U.T. Trolleybuses. The London street scene shown above has its counterpart in big cities all over the globe . . . for B.U.T. are supplying nearly two-thirds of British-built trolleybuses for service at home and abroad. Write for particulars of the full range of B.U.T. models . . . the "Best Under Test."

See them on **STAND 31** at the
**COMMERCIAL VEHICLE EXHIBITION · EARLS COURT**

A·E·C LEYLAND TROLLEYBUSES

## B.U.T. TROLLEYBUSES
*The Senior Silent Service*

**BRITISH UNITED TRACTION LIMITED**
HANOVER HOUSE · HANOVER SQUARE · LONDON, W.1

**British United Traction have taken space in transport magazines advertising their wares. The image of 1675 wa taken in Grays Inn Road, with the photograph of 109 being in Charterhouse Street.**

---

### Re-allocation of Trolleybus Routes 2819

**Notice to Inspectors and Conductors—Holloway and Finchley Depots**

Commencing on Wednesday, 29th October, 1941, Routes 517/617, now operating from Finchley depot will operate from Holloway depot, and Route 609 now operating from Finchley depot on Sundays only will operate from that depot throughout the week. Specimens of altered tickets and farebills will be exhibited in the depots and attention is drawn to the two 4d. workman return tickets at Finchley depot, one for use on Route 609 and the other on Routes 521/621.
The 8d. and 9d. single tickets for use on Route 609 will be entered on the waybills in spaces allocated to 1½d. single transfer and 2½d. single tickets respectively.

**Destination Blinds**

Alterations have been made to front and rear blinds at both depots, and the following wording must be shown :—

**Transfer Fares**

Attention is called to the ordinary single transfers at 4d., 5d. and 6d. issued on routes 517/617 between Tally Ho Corner and Holborn Loop and intermediately. Workman return tickets issued for journeys from Holborn Loop, Guilford Street or Farringdon Road, Rosebery Avenue, are available for transfer on the return journey at Nag's Head, Holloway.

**Alternative Return Journey**

Workman return tickets issued on Routes 521/621 for journeys between Holborn Loop, Guilford Street or Rosebery Avenue, Farringdon Road, Offord Road or Nag's Head and Tally Ho Corner are available for return on Route 517/617 between the points of issue. This facility does not operate so that tickets issued on Route 517/617 are available for return on Route 521/621.

| Depot | When Running to | Route | Show No. | Show Wording |
|---|---|---|---|---|
| Holloway .. .. | Holborn .. .. .. .. | 517 | 22 | via Grays Inn Road HOLBORN CIRCUS |
| ,, .. .. | ,, | 617 | 23 | HOLBORN CIRCUS via Farringdon Road |
| ,, .. .. | North Finchley .. .. | 517/617 | 24 | NORTH FINCHLEY via Highgate |
| ,, .. .. | King's Cross .. .. .. | 517/617 | 21 | KING'S CROSS |
| Finchley .. .. | East Finchley Station .. .. | 609 | 18 | EAST FINCHLEY STATION |
| ,, .. .. | Windsor Terrace, City Road .. | 609 | 19 | Windsor Terrace CITY ROAD |

Almost at the bottom of Grays Inn Road L3 1474 on the 621 heads for North Finchley. On the opposite side of the road and with its blind already changed for North Finchley but on the 521 is L3 1521; its registration numerals and route numbers match. The photographer would have no idea at the time that he would be chasing 1521 around the Twickenham, Teddington and Kingston areas in his father's car in the afternoon of 8th May 1962 during its trip for local dignitaries. That night he would be in and around Kingston and Fulwell, prolifically photographing 1521 as it became the last trolleybus to operate in the capital.

*Peter Moore*

Well before any trolleybus incursion into Grays Inn Road five tramcars are seen at its southern end. The only one identifiable is Feltham 2068 which has its blind set for North Finchley on route 21. It was a stipulation in the inner parts of London that trams operate in conduit mode.

L3 1462 is by Baldwins Gardens – a few hundred yards before the end of Grays Inn Road. It is working on route 521 to Holborn Circus on 6th May 1961. Two motorbuses follow the trolleybus.
*Peter Mitchell 17190*

Open-fronted tram 1056 has just arrived at its Holborn terminus in Grays Inn Road; the blind is set for a return to Stamford Hill on route 43. Trolleybus overhead can be seen above E1 1056 whose days are therefore numbered.
*H. B. Priestley*

A major fault of underground trolleybus cabling occurred in Grays Inn Road during the evening of 16th December 1954; breakdown crews are on the scene, sorting the problem out. The hold-up occurred somewhere between Kings Cross and Holborn. It is not known if vehicles moved through normally, or if the power was switched off and they passed by on battery with their booms on the overhead. Trolleybuses are still operating both ways around the Holborn Loop.

*London Transport Museum U57237/57239*

Trolleybus route 617 was inaugurated on 6th March 1938; tram route 3 was withdrawn on 9th July 1938 so this view at the tram stub at the bottom of Grays Inn Road was taken between these times. H1 768 works on route 617 to North Finchley while E class open fronted car 538 will soon set off to Hampstead on route 3. In the far distance another tram can be made out; 768 is about to overtake some workers who may be carrying out tram track repairs.
*London Transport Museum U2557*

Trainee trolleybus drivers had to be familiar with overhead wiring on all routes from the depot to which they would be allocated. At Highgate they would drive in the City of London which 1421 is about to do; it turns from Grays Inn Road into Holborn. One of the four entrances to Chancery Lane underground station is on the left.
*Bill Godwin*

768 was allocated to Holloway depot from new; it moves from Holborn into Grays Inn Road while working on the
617 to North Finchley. The two white panels on the destination blind are markers to assist conductors and drivers
to correctly position the displays; they were soon replaced by 'tell-tale' stickers on the back of the blinds.  768's
destination blinds (front and rear) were conductor-operated.                          *London Transport Museum H16057*

With Staple Inn in th background 1431 has move from Holborn into Grays In Road on the last day of rout 613 - 31st January 1961. L 1431 became the penultimat trolleybus to operate i London - on 8th May 1962 when it preceded 1521 int Fulwell depot.     *Brian Spelle*

517s/617s were sometime curtailed at East Finchle station. 1574's crew hav been instructed to turn ther on 24th December 1960 - Christmas traffic is probabl the cause of delaying this 617 An entrance to Chancery Lane Station on the left ha a typical **UNDERGROUND** bullseye symbol.     *Lyndon Row*

---

# COMMENDATIONS

**MR. F. E. SKELLEY**
Conductor No. 5169
Holloway Depot

*From* Ernest Ruthen,
A.R.I.B.A., F.S.I.

No. 1, Kings Mews,
Bloomsbury,
London, W.C.1

2nd October, 1946

Dear Sir,

I travelled down Grays Inn Road at 11.30 o'clock this morning on a No. 513 trolleybus, and I noticed the particular and nice way which the conductor executed his duties. Apart from that, his manner and appearance was a credit to your Department, and in my view, from many years experience of travelling around London, this conductor is one who could be put up as a model. I wrote his number down (i.e. 5169) unawares to him.

Yours faithfully,
(Signed) ERNEST RUTHEN

---

LETTERS OF COMMENDATION HAVE ALSO BEEN RECEIVED REGARDING :

| | | | | |
|---|---|---|---|---|
| Mr. G. T. FAGGETTER | ... | Conductor ... | ... No. 4243 ... | Fullwell Depot |
| Miss E. G. KIPLING | ... | W/Conductor ... | ... No. 7599 ... | Bow Depot |
| Mrs. A. PEACH | ... ... | W/Conductor ... | ... No. 11458 ... | Abbey Wood Depot |

L3 1482 on the 521 is in Holborn and by the Prudential building on 6th May 1961; although the driver has changed the destination blind to show North Finchley, 1482 still heads towards Holborn Circus. Trolleybuses do not stop in Holborn and therefore do not recognise the compulsory bus stop on the right. In this vicinity ten traction poles' length of overhead was within the City of London. *Peter Mitchell 17188*

An animated view in Holborn with K1 1127 on route 543 centre stage; the driver has already changed the destination blind to show **WOOD GREEN STN.** A lot of pedestrians walk by and motor traffic passes in both directions; parking in the middle of the road is not a new phenomenon. Many street furniture items are in position. *Denis Battams*

On the opposite side of the road Edmonton's 1188 has just started its long northbound trip to Waltham Cross on the 659 on 3rd July 1960; as with the 500 series routes the 600 set of routes did not stop in Holborn. Passing Prince Albert's statue is K2 1225 which moves out of Charterhouse Street into Holborn on route 643 on 13th May 1961; L3 1465 on the 621 makes the same manoeuvre on 10th June 1961.

*Peter Mitchell*
*15378/17271/18002*

L3 1431 moves from Holborn into Charterhouse Street on 31st December 1961; it is working on route 513 and shows VIA KENTISH TOWN FORTESS WALK. Bearing in mind that Holborn is a central part of London it seems incongruous that such an obscure side street as FORTESS WALK was shown from there. With no relieving crew at Fortess Walk, 1431 will temporarily be removed from the service. *Jack Gready*

Destination blinds front, rear and side on Routes Nos. 513/613 must be turned on the inward journey after crossing Clerkenwell Road and before arriving at either Holborn, Grays Inn Road or Farringdon Street Station.

**Luggage on Trolleybuses.**

Only personal luggage of a nature not likely to be dangerous or objectionable to passengers or to damage the vehicle or impede the conductor in his duty will be permitted. No charge will be made.

th January 1961 was a Saturday, not the day of the week for inner-city trolleybus routes to experience heavy passenger loadings; K1 1267 on route 513 moves from Holborn into Charterhouse Street. The driver has already set the destination blind for its next trip to Parliament Hill Fields. *Lyndon Rowe*

| Route No. | Turning Points |
|---|---|
| 513/ 613 | Parliament Hill Fields (clockwise) |
| | Hampstead, South End Green (clockwise) |
| | Highgate Road, Fortess Road anti-clockwise) |
| | *Prince of Wales Road, 'Mother Shipton' (clockwise) battery |
| | Kings Cross, Swinton Street (anti-clockwise) |
| | Clerkenwell Green (clockwise) |

Entering Charterhouse Street is a smart-looking M1 1553 which also had its blind changed before arriving there – to North Finchley on the 517. In the background work is in progress in constructing the Daily Mirror building. *Roy Hubble*

The Daily Mirror building has been completed and many of its windows are open on a hot Tuesday 18th July 1961, the last day of route 643; it is 1264's final ever service trip. From Charterhouse Street it will head back to Stamford Hill depot. K1 1264 had been a recent addition to SF stock, having arrived on 9th June 1961.

*Don Lewis*

Within a month 1264 was sold for scrap to George Cohen & Co. It is the first of three K class vehicles that have made their own way from Fulwell works to arrive at the entrance to Colindale scrapyard on 17th August 1961 - their date of sale. Second in line is 1227, then 1339. Cohen's staff will move them into the yard later in the day; by the end of the month all three will probably have been dismantled.

*Tony Belton*

Pages 171 to 174 show vehicles working clockwise around Holborn loop.

Top) B2 116 is on route 613 to Hampstead Heath. Middle and lower) 1361 and 1412 are both 617s; L1 1361 is only going to Highgate – L3 1412 is going the full length of the route to North Finchley. Both have slipped route numbers, a common sight on Highgate's vehicles; 1361 has a paper route blind, 1412 a linen one. Note the Metropolitan Police **NO WAITING** sign.

*Top photo Don Jones,*
*second and third images*
*Don Lewis*

Edmonton depot was the sol operator of route 659; K 1080 waits in Charterhous Street. The police would no allow trolleybuses to stan here; however, it was neithe obeyed or enforced by then or inspectors – it was jus not practical for vehicle to go 'in and out' as regula service intervals could no have been maintained. To th rear of 1080 is X5 1379 which is unusually seen working o route 617. *Don Jone*

K2 1220 looks odd without trolleybus 'bullseye' symbo on its front panel; the nudit was introduced as a financia economy on overhaule vehicles in 1952. There wa bad feed-back from passenger and staff; the 'bullseye' soo returned to its revered an proper place. 1220 waits ou time before setting off for trip on route 643. Note tha on this and the previous pag an inspector is positioned t ensure efficient running.
*Alan Cros*

K1 1090 on route 659 is parke behind another trolleybu in Charterhouse Street – i is a busy time of day as tw others are in front. 1090's rea destination blind shows half o each terminus – **WALTHAN CROSS** and **HOLBORN CIRCUS**. Has the blind slippe or has the conductor save himself some blind-windin by deliberately showing a 'ha and half' display? *Roy Hubbl*

t was unusual for trolleybuses to overtake one another in Charterhouse Street. In this instance though, the crew f J1 946 on the 621 have removed its poles from the overhead and rested them against a span wire to allow J2 016 on the 617 to overtake. Both are going to North Finchley – it is quicker and cheaper to travel there by 617. t is 14th September 1959.

*Norman Rayfield*

Only four trolleybus routes served Holborn Circus when this view was taken on 3rd June 1961. With a lesser umber of routes and less frequent services on Saturdays it was unusual to see one vehicle 'dip its sticks' for nother. However, this occurred on this day with K2 1213 on route 643 overtaking L3 1507 on route 621. The ompulsory stop now includes a facility to use E plate route numbers – trolleybus only though! See picture of 1220 n the previous page.

*Hugh Taylor*

J1 950 turns from Farringdon Road into Charterhouse Street on 6th June 1938, exactly three months to the day since route 621 commenced; in the background is Smithfield Meat Market with a number of vans and lorries parked beneath its canopies. A few minutes later J2 976, on the 617, makes the same manoeuvre but is only going as far as **HIGHGATE ARCHWAY TAVERN**; as 'shorts' to Archway were only scheduled on the 517 the most likely scenario here is that 976 is running into Holloway depot having first traversed Archway loop.

*London Transport Museum U27410/2741*

When this photograph was taken, route 565 operated in Monday to Friday peak hours and even then, only at fifteen-minute intervals. Although there are images of them in and around Poplar depot this is the only one known of a 565 in passenger service. Mr Wellings was a bank messenger and often took his camera to work; he had an ambition of photographing every motorbus and trolleybus route in London. N2 1657 is on Charterhouse Street stand sometime in October 1953; it is running into West Ham depot at the end of the morning peak hour. It shows **WEST HAM GREENGATE ST**. This was the display that vehicles on the Barking Road services showed when running into **WH**.

*Ron Wellings*

It is 3.37pm on Sunday 3rd July 1960. Although there was no commercial or business activity in Central London on that day of the week, Charterhouse Street seems far more deserted than might be expected. There is no other vehicle in sight as Finchley's 1486 on the 521 passes Ely Place.

*Peter Mitchell 15380*

# VEHICLE TIME CARD

## 7236 — HAMPSTEAD or PARLIAMENT HILL FIELDS and HOLBORN CIRCUS — ROUTES 513/6

SCHEDULE NUMBER **7236**
OPERATING ON **XMAS DAY 25.12.54** LEAVE DEPOT **8.53**
RUNNING NUMBER **HT 4**

| Hampstead | Kings X via Grays Inn Rd. | Holborn | Kings X | Fortess Walk | SWAINS LANE Arrive | SWAINS LANE Leave | Fortess Walk | Kings X via Farringdon Rd. | Holborn | Kings X | Hampstead |
|---|---|---|---|---|---|---|---|---|---|---|---|
| | | | | | | | | | | | 9.8 |
| 9.10 | 9.25 | 9.32 | | | | | | | 9.32 | 9.39 | 9.53 |
| 10.0 | 10.15 | 10.22 | | | | | | | 10.22 | 10.29 | 10.43 |
| 10.50 | 11.5 | 11.12 | | | | | | | 11.12 | 11.19 | 11.33 |
| 11.40 | 11.55 | 12.2 | | | | | | | 12.2 | 12.10 | 12.26 |
| 12.30 | 12.45 | 12.52 | | | | | | | 12.52 | 1.0 | 1.14 |
| 1.20 | 1.35 | 1.42 | | | | | | | 1.42 | 1.50 | 2.4 |
| 2.10 | 2.25 | 2.32 | | | | | | | 2.32 | 2.40 | 2.54 |
| 3.0 | 3.15 | 3.22 | | | | | | | 3.22 | 3.30 | |
| | | | | | | | | DEPOT 3.47 | | | |

---

# VEHICLE TIME CARD

## 7351 — NORTH FINCHLEY and HOLBORN CIRCUS via HIGHGATE — ROUTES 517/6 — SUPP

TIME SCHEDULE NUMBER **7351**
OPERATING ON **GOOD FRIDAY. 8-4-55** LEAVE DEPOT **7.13**
RUNNING NUMBER **HT 10**

| North Finchley | East Finchley Station | Salisbury Road | Archway Station | Nags Head (P&H BERTON GDNS) | KINGS CROSS via Grays Inn | KINGS CROSS via Farringdon | SWINTON STREET Arrive | SWINTON STREET Leave | Holborn | Kings Cross | Nags Head (P&H BERTON GDNS) | Archway Station | Salisbury Road | East Finchley Station | North Finchley |
|---|---|---|---|---|---|---|---|---|---|---|---|---|---|---|---|
| | | | | | | | | | | | 7.15 | 7.18 | | | 7.34 |
| 7.39 | | | 7.57 | | 8.12 | | 8.14 | 8.20 | | 8.22 | 8.37 | | | | 8.55 |
| 8.59 | | | 9.17 | | 9.32 | | 9.34 | 9.38 | | 9.40 | 9.55 | | | | 10.13 |
| 10.19 | | | 10.37 | 10.40 | | DEPOT 10.42 | | | | | | | | | |
| | | | | | | | | | DEPOT 11.34 | | 11.36 | 11.39 | | | 11.57 |
| 12.3 | | | 12.21 | | 12.36 | | 12.38 | 12.42 | | 12.44 | 12.50 | | | | 1.17 |
| 1.23 | | | 1.41 | | 1.56 | | 1.58 | 2.2 | | 2.4 | 2.19 | 21 | | | |
| | | | 2.23 | 2.24 | 2.27 | DEPOT 2.29 | | | | | | | | | |

**Early Morning Single Fares Available Up To 8 a.m. To ARCHWAY STATION**

**BUS RUNS LIGHT ON JOURNEYS UNDERLINED**

These three views show trolleybuses operating on the Holborn anti-clockwise loop. K2A 1247A is allocated to Highgate depot and on route 517; front advertisements are yet to be fitted. J1 928 is on route 521 despite showing 621 in its route box aperture. A few yards further down Charterhouse Street K1A 1123A is on route 543 and the first in a line-up of three trolleybuses parked up.

*Don Jones*

1305 was allocated to running number SF17 on route 543 on Tuesday 18th July 1961, the last day of the route. I̶
was running late in the morning and an inspector curtailed it to Shoreditch, thus allowing the crew to come off o̶
time. Sometime later in the day it was placed on SF4 where it is photographed in Charterhouse Street at 8.06pm̶
This is the last ever 543; when it gets to Stamford Hill there will be a crew change and on arrival at Wood Gree̶
the conductor will change all route details to show route 643, which it will display until it runs into Stamford Hi̶
depot later in the evening. Note the 243 Monday to Saturday E plate on the bus stop flag ready for the next da̶

*Peter Mitchell 1837*

## LOG SHEET

ST/HILL GARAGE  DATE 18-7-61
ROUTE NUMBER 643  VEHICLE NUMBER 1305  RUNNING NUMBER 17

| Point | Arr. time | Dep. time | Point | Arr. time | Dep. time |
|---|---|---|---|---|---|
| ST/HILL DEP. | 7.40 | 7.45 | WOOD GREEN | 8.5 | 8.10 |
| HOLBORN | 8.55 | | " | 9.46 | 9.53 |
| SHORED | 9.54 | 10.41 | ST/HILL | 11.13 | |

| Left garage | Time | Inspector's initials | Arrived garage | Time | Inspector's initials |
|---|---|---|---|---|---|
| | 7.40 AM | | | | |

PASSENGERS TRANSFERRED FROM OTHER VEHICLES

| Route No. | Running No. | Ticket machine No. | Total register No. at start of trip |
|---|---|---|---|
| | | | |

402/60 (5)
(800m-7/60-D20-Stock)

### STAFF DETAILS

| Duty No. | Grade | Name | Badge number | Time taking over | Time relieved on previous bus | Ticket machine number | Total reg. No. at start of last trip | Duty No. | Grade | Name | Badge number | Time taking over | Time relieved on previous bus | Ticket machine number | Total reg. No. at start of last trip |
|---|---|---|---|---|---|---|---|---|---|---|---|---|---|---|---|
| 44 | Dr. | WOOD | 11574 | 740 | | 826/10 | 848 | | Dr. | | | | | | |
| | Cr. | RABIN | 17767 | 7.40 | | | | | Cr. | | | | | | |
| | Dr. | | | | | | | | Dr. | | | | | | |
| | Cr. | | | | | | | | Cr. | | | | | | |
| | Dr. | | | | | | | | Dr. | | | | | | |
| | Cr. | | | | | | | | Cr. | | | | | | |
| | Dr. | | | | | | | | Dr. | | | | | | |
| | Cr. | | | | | | | | Cr. | | | | | | |

### CURTAILMENTS, INVOLUNTARY STOPS AND TRAFFIC DELAYS

| Where delayed | TIME Stopped | TIME Resumed | Cause of delay | JOURNEY OR PART JOURNEY LOST From | To | AUTHORIZED BY OFFICIAL Time | Signature | No. | IF BUS CHANGED Place | Vehicle No. 2nd bus | Initials of driver |
|---|---|---|---|---|---|---|---|---|---|---|---|
| | | | | SHOREDITCH | | | | 10/53 | S | | |

This is the log card for K2 1305 operating on route 543 on 18th July 1961 - the last day of the route.

TROLLEYBUSES

Sold to Messrs. G. Cohen Ltd., Fulwell

1212, 1225, 1237, (30.8.61.)
1245, 1305, 1695, (31.8.61.)

Recording of Failures,    483
Delays and Lost Mileage

Staff are notified that as from Wednesday, 26th April, 1950 the present method of entering lost or excess miles on the record of Deviations from Scheduled Car Miles, (Form No. D.40/412/39) will be discontinued.

From that date a log sheet (Form No. D.40/402/60 (4)-D) will be used for each vehicle and will be issued to the conductor working the first journey, and will be retained on that vehicle throughout the day and passed from one conductor to the other, being finally handed in by the conductor working the last journey. If, for any reason, the crew have to leave a vehicle whilst still in service the log sheet must be left with the time Card. Provision is made on these log sheets for arrival and departure times from terminal points. Part or complete journeys lost, and excess journeys, and all delays must be recorded by the conductor whilst on the vehicle. This will avoid the necessity for recording these items at the termination of the day's work.

Although they worked on 'The Hampstead routes' on a daily basis it was highly unusual to see a B3 photographed at Holborn Circus terminus - 485 is there one day on route 513. An 'odd' feature is that it is fitted with 'paper' route and destination blinds, meaning it could work on any of Highgate's main routes and possibly why it is so attired. Withdrawn in February 1955 it was not sold until April 1956 – for scrap to Bird's of Stratford-upon-Avon.

J2 1016 loads up at the bottom of Charterhouse Street ready for a trip to Parliament Hill Fields on the 513. Oddly, a bus stop flag and dolly stop are positioned together.
*Roy Hubble*

K1 1066 was transferred from Walthamstow to Highgate depot at stage five of the conversion scheme; it stayed there four more stages, being withdrawn on the night of 31st January 1961. It is 3rd July 1960 and the crew wait out time at Charterhouse Street before departure to Hampstead Heath on route 513.
*Peter Mitchell 15379*

### Battery Charging                    2696

**Notice to Drivers**

Constant running of the motor generators for battery charging causes serious damage and drivers are instructed that the M.G. sets must not be used during daylight, except when the batteries have failed to turn the trolleybus, or for any other reason the amount of current in the battery is found to be inadequate.

The M.G. Set must not be run before taking the trolleybus into service, nor after the vehicle has completed the day's run, merely for the purpose of charging up the battery.

**On 31st January 1961 - the last day of route 517 - K2 1330 moves out of Charterhouse Street and into Farringdon Road. Going the other way is K2 1236 on the 659 - three other trolleybuses are behind it**

*Clarence Carter.*
*Roy Hubble*

### Flashing from Overhead           2718

Drivers must make every effort to stop flashing during the hours of darkness. This will be prevented by cutting off current before crossing breaks in the overhead wires. White bands on the poles indicate where these breaks occur.

**J2 1017 moves from Farringdon Road into Charterhouse Street while working on route 617; the reduced depth destination blind is clearly not fit for the job as the glass has not been masked and indicates that 1017 is travelling simultaneously via Grays Inn Road and Farringdon Road!**

*Roy Hubble*

K2 1223 is in Farringdon Road on 6th May 1961 on route 643; in about 150 yards it will turn into Charterhouse Street where it will pause for a short while before heading north. 1223 only ever operated out of Stamford Hill depot.

*Peter Mitchell 17193*

E1 tramcar 1059 is at the Farringdon Road terminus of route 17. As mentioned on page 78, an error at Charlton Works saw **FARRINGDON ST** produced on Holloway's tram blinds rather than **FARRINGDON RD.** Trolleybus overhead is in place for the tram/trolleybus change-over of 6th March 1938.

The photographer was principally a 'tram man' but there were times when he was involved with trolleybuses. In this instance he is near the Clerkenwell Road / Farringdon Road overhead junction where Farringdon Road book market was held; a passer-by has a browse while a 613 heads for Holborn Circus. The frog hand pull on the traction pole on the left is for 543s heading to Stamford Hill and 565s going to Barking.

*J. H. Price*

**In pouring rain, L3 1489 on the 521 has dewired at the junction of Clerkenwell Road with Farringdon Road; both booms left the overhead at the Farringdon Road facing frog. Conductor and driver are attending to the situation. Although all dewirements were to be reported, it is doubtful this one was – no officials around!** *Robert Jowett*

FARES

ROUTE 565—BARKING — ALDGATE — HOLBORN (F.T.2180) (Aug. 1956)
ROUTE 567—BARKING — ALDGATE — SMITHFIELD
ROUTE 665—BARKING — ALDGATE — BLOOMSBURY

✶ NEW FARE STAGES
17–Trinity Church
15–Iron Bridge Tavern
13–Poplar Baths
10–Exmouth Street
3–Holborn Hall

†–Farezone

| West India Docks–14 | Stage Point No. | | | | | | | | | | | | | | | | | | | | | Stage |
|---|---|---|---|---|---|---|---|---|---|---|---|---|---|---|---|---|---|---|---|---|---|---|
| | 23 | | | | | | | | | | | | | | | | | | | | | Barking Terminus–23 |
| | 22 | 2½ | | | | | | | | | | | | | | | | | | | | Burges Road–22 |
| | 21 | 2½ | 2½ | | | | | | | | | | | | | | | | | | | East Ham Town Hall–21 |
| | 20 | 4 | 2½ | 2½ | | | | | | | | | | | | | | | | | | Barking Road, Green Street–20 |
| | 19 | 4 | 4 | 2½ | 2½ | | | | | | | | | | | | | | | | | Greengate Street–19 |
| | 18 | 6 | 4 | 4 | 2½ | 2½ | | | | | | | | | | | | | | | | Balaam Street–18 |
| | 17 | 6 | 6 | 4 | 4 | 2½ | 2½ | | | | | | | | | | | | | | | Trinity Church–17 ✶ |
| | 16 | 6 | 6 | 4 | 4 | 2½ | 2½ | 2½ | | | | | | | | | | | | | | Canning Town Station–16 |
| | 15 | 8 | 6 | 6 | 4 | 4 | 2½ | 2½ | 2½ | | | | | | | | | | | | | Iron Bridge Tavern–15 ✶ |
| | 14 | 8 | 8 | 6 | 6 | 4 | 4 | 2½ | 2½ | 2½ | | | | | | | | | | | | Blackwall Tunnel–14 |
| | 13 | 8 | 8 | 6 | 6 | 4 | 4 | 4 | 2½ | 2½ | 2½ | | | | | | | | | | | Poplar Baths–13 ✶ |
| 2½ | 12 | 10 | 8 | 8 | 6 | 6 | 6 | 4 | 4 | 4 | 2½ | 2½ | | | | | | | | | | Burdett Road–12 |
| 2½ | 11 | 10 | 10 | 8 | 8 | 6 | 6 | 6 | 4 | 4 | 4 | 2½ | 2½ | | | | | | | | | Stepney East Station–11 |
| 4 | 10 | 1/- | 10 | 10 | 8 | 8 | 8 | 6 | 6 | 6 | 4 | 4 | 2½ | 2½ | | | | | | | | Exmouth Street–10 ✶ |
| 4 | 9 | 1/- | 1/- | 10 | 10 | 8 | 8 | 8 | 6 | 6 | 6 | 4 | 4 | 2½ | 2½ | | | | | | | New Road–9 |
| 4 | 8 | 1/2 | 1/- | 1/- | 10 | 10 | 8 | 8 | 8 | 8 | 6 | 6 | 4 | 4 | 2½ | 2½ | | | | | | Gardiners Corner–8 |
| 6 | 7 | 1/2 | 1/2 | 1/- | 1/- | 10 | 10 | 10 | 8 | 8 | 8 | 6 | 6 | 4 | 4 | 2½ | 2½ | | | | | Shoreditch High Street–7† |
| 6 | 6 | 1/4 | 1/2 | 1/2 | 1/- | 1/- | 10 | 10 | 10 | 10 | 8 | 8 | 6 | 6 | 4 | 4 | 2½ | 2½ | | | | Old Street, City Road–6 |
| 8 | 5 | 1/4 | 1/4 | 1/2 | 1/2 | 1/- | 1/- | 1/- | 10 | 10 | 10 | 8 | 8 | 6 | 6 | 4 | 4 | 2½ | 2½ | | | Goswell Road–5 |
| 8 | 4 | 1/4 | 1/4 | 1/2 | 1/2 | 1/2 | 1/- | 1/- | 1/- | 1/- | 10 | 10 | 8 | 8 | 6 | 6 | 4 | 4 | 2½ | 2½ | | Grays Inn Road, Holborn Circus or Farringdon Stn.–4 |
| 8 | 3 | 1/4 | 1/4 | 1/2 | 1/2 | 1/2 | 1/- | 1/- | 1/- | 1/- | 10 | 10 | 8 | 8 | 6 | 6 | 4 | 4 | 2½ | 2½ | | Holborn Hall–3 ✶ |
| 8 | 2 | 1/4 | 1/4 | 1/2 | 1/2 | 1/2 | 1/- | 1/- | 1/- | 1/- | 10 | 10 | 10 | 8 | 8 | 6 | 6 | 4 | 4 | 2½ | 2½ | Bloomsbury, Red Lion Square (Route 665)–2 |
| 8 | 1 | 1/4 | 1/4 | 1/2 | 1/2 | 1/2 | 1/- | 1/- | 1/- | 1/- | 10 | 10 | 8 | 8 | 6 | 6 | 4 | 4 | 2½ | 2½ | | Smithfield (Route 567)–1 |
| 4 | 8 | 1/2 | 1/- | 1/- | 10 | 10 | 8 | 8 | 8 | 8 | 6 | 6 | 4 | 4 | 2½ | 2½ | | | | | | Aldgate Station (Route 567)–8 |

EARLY MORNING SINGLE FARES

| Where the Ordinary Single fare is | Early Morning Single fare will be |
|---|---|
| 8d. – 1/4 | 7d. |

An animated scene at the junction of Clerkenwell Road with Farringdon Road; the subjects are L3 1498 on the 521 and K1 1112 on the 543. There is a lot of vehicle and pedestrian activity including one man about to step onto the pavement.    *Tony Belton*

The photographer has pointed his camera skywards to capture on film as much as possible of the cat's cradle of overhead at the Farringdon Road/Clerkenwell Road junction on 24th October 1959. This overhead layout did not change in any form between February 1939 and July 1961.
*John Gillham*

These views of trolleybuse[s] working clockwise around the Holborn loop were taken a[t] the junction of Clerkenwel[l] Road with Farringdon Road[.] N2 1668 is on route 613 o[n] 31st December 1960 whil[e] K3 1672 is on route 659 o[n] 20th April 1961. Two vehicle[s] going in the opposite directio[n] are of interest: one has th[e] registration number of 4 APF[,] while the vehicle behind it i[s] nicknamed a 'Woody'.

*Jack Gready*

| F.2944 | Farringdon Rd (E), Vine St. Bridge | 16. 8.38 | Clockwise via Farringdon Rd. (E), Vine St. Bridge and Farringdon Road. | Emergency only. |
|---|---|---|---|---|

A short way to the east i[s] Clerkenwell Green loop; thi[s] view of its trailing frog ha[s] only just surfaced and show[s] it better than the shot of it i[n] the previous book in the serie[s;] the facing frog is also see[n.] All the overhead seen her[e] remained in use until 18th Jul[y] 1961. This view was taken o[n] 24th October 1959 while JC[G] was photographing route[s] that would be withdrawn afte[r] 10th November 1959.

*John Gillhan[*]

184

J1 908 on the 621 leads a 659 through Clerkenwell Road/Farringdon Road junction. The most interesting feature in this view is the trailing frog out of Vine Street into Farringdon Road; this shortworking was never shown on destination blinds. The loop's wiring was removed by October 1956.

*Don Thompson*

Due to tram track removal in Rosebery Avenue, trolleybuses on route 581 were diverted in both directions for some weeks in 1953. In the top image, on 25th April 1953, K2 1353 is using a temporary link which allowed them to move from Farringdon Road into Clerkenwell Road where they joined line of route at the bottom end of Rosebery Avenue; going the other way 581s continued along Clerkenwell Road, turned left at Goswell Road and used 677 wires to Angel Islington where line of route was picked up. The lower photo shows ironwork being removed from Rosebery Avenue on 5th April 1953; buses and trolleybuses are unable to traverse this street but it looks as if cars can.

*Clarence Carter*

By Farringdon Road Goods depot, E1 car 1066 is ready to return to Highgate on route 17. This service terminated at the end of Farringdon Road so 1066 has been turned short of its destination.  *W. A. Camwell*

Edmonton depot had a smattering of H1s over the years; latterly they were the higher numbered vehicles of the class. Seen in Farringdon Road opposite Cowcross Street and by Farringdon Road goods depot on 7th May 1955 is 895 with a badly positioned destination blind; it heads for Holborn Circus on route 659.

*Peter Mitchell 7172*

| | | |
|---|---|---|
| 11.45 | FARRINGDON:                         2868 | |
| | Central Bus Controller reported that Bus Service no. 63 had been diverted. | |
| | North Trolleybus Controller reported that Trolleybus Services 513, 613, 521, 621, and 659, | |
| 11.46 | were being turned back. | |
| 11.47 | Three trolleybuses, numbers as below, received minor damage by blast:- | |
| |      No. 959, on Service    621. | |
| |      " 1162,   do.    659. | |
| 13.45 |      " 1205,   do.    643. | |
| | One driver and one conductor suffered from shock. | |
| 13.50 | | |

| | | |
|---|---|---|
| Fri. 9.3.45 | | |
| 07.50 | FARRINGDON:                         2868. | |
| | Chiswick Control reported the following damage to buses:- | |
| |     Petrol Bus    STL.1972.     on Service 22 - | |
| |                               two windows blasted. | |
| |       Do.     STL.1741.     on Service 12 - | |
| |                               one window blasted. | |
| |         Two passengers injured. | |
| 08.15 | North Trolleybus Controller stated that one track of the Holborn loop was re-opened at 07.30 | |
| | hours. | |
| | Services 513, 517, 521, 543, and 565 were running through on one track. | |

**War damage reports for 8th/9th March 1945.**

Taken from a crouching position K2 1168 passed through the Farringdon Road / Rosebery Avenue crossover on 22nd May 1955, while working on route 659; seen from a standing stance J1 943 waited at the traffic lights there on 8th April 1959 while working on route 621. There had been a non-traffic link between Rosebery Avenue and Farringdon Road since June 1939; it was removed in March 1947. The facility was restored for a few weeks in 1953 when route 581 was diverted along Farringdon Road. The News of the World advertisement was a permanent feature here for many years.

*Don Thompson*
*John Clark*

K1 1105 led a chequered life during the trolleybus conversion programme. It moved from Walthamstow to Hanwell at stage five (February 1960); withdrawn from HL in November 1960 (stage eight) it was reinstated to Highgate depot the following month. Withdrawn from HT at the end of January 1961 (stage nine) a further reinstatement saw it return to its original depot of Stamford Hill in March 1961; it did not survive stage eleven (July 1961) and was scrapped soon afterwards. With Clerkenwell fire station in the background and where Farringdon Road crosses Rosebery Avenue 1105 heads for North Finchley on route 517; L3 1456 on route 521 follows going to the same location but by a longer route.

*Tony Belton*

544 on route 621 is opposite the **GPO** sorting office in Farringdon Road on 28th October 1961; the side entrance
o Mount Pleasant headquarters is in this street - the main one is in Rosebery Avenue. 1544's advertisement panels
uggest people purchase Haig whisky for Christmas. As it will be withdrawn on 8th November the adverts are
oing to be out of use very soon; didn't the publicity department have details of vehicles' withdrawal dates and act
ccordingly? NO.                                                                                           *Peter Mitchell 19412*

:1 1148 is by Attneave Street which is off Farringdon Road; it is going to Holborn Circus on route 659 on 23rd July
960. There was never a comparable anti-clockwise service to Waltham Cross.                    *Peter Mitchell 15567*

1463 was transferred from West Ham to Finchley depot on 3rd February 1960 working on route 621 it is in Kings Cross Road by Cubbitt Street on 6th May 1961. At stage twelve of the conversion scheme the fifteen lowest numbered Finchley L3s in the best condition in the 1449-1469 series were retained until stage thirteen. 1463 and 1467 did not fall into that category so were withdrawn and sent to Colindale depot for storage; both went for scrap on 14th December 1961.

*Peter Mitchell 1718*

1460, a 621 to Holborn Circus is in Kings Cross Road by Wharton Street on 5th March 1961. It spent most of its life at Poplar and West Ham depots it moved from WH to Finchley at stage six of the conversion scheme and stayed until 2nd January 1962 when it was sent to Fulwell unlicensed. There was no rush to dispose of 1460 and it hung around in Fulwell works until 18th April 1962.

*Peter Mitchell 1683*

1452 has moved out of Swinton Street and into Kings Cross Road and is by the intriguingly named Great Percy Street on the final leg of its trip to Holborn Circus on the 621 on 2nd September 1961; L3 1452 has exactly four months of service in front of it as it will be withdrawn on 2nd January 1962.

*Peter Mitchell 18782*

Further along Kings Cross Road is L1 1364 on route 517 to North Finchley on 31st December 1960. This is not an interesting area but shows that trolleybuses operate in mundane places as well. Many crates of milk bottles have been left on the pavement. *Jack Gready*

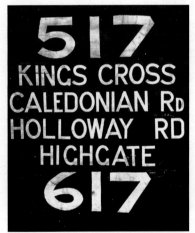

This is the Kings Cross Road facing frog. Nearby a shop quotes ELB – many a trolleybus with that combination of registration letters has passed by. *John Gillham*

JI 951 on route 521 has jus[t] passed through the facing fro[g] in Kings Cross Road wher[e] trolleybuses heading toward[s] Kings Cross and North Finchle[y] diverged. A large quantity o[f] boxes is dumped outside Presan[t] & Fisher Ltd. *Fred Ive[y]*

At the bottom of Pentonvill[e] Road (Caledonian Road is to th[e] left) on 31st December 1960 i[s] L3 1431 on route 513. The drive[r] is about to pass through man[y] items of 'special work' before h[e] gets to 'easier wiring' in Pancra[s] Road. 1431 had worked at Popla[r] and West Ham depots unt[il] transferred to Highgate at stag[e] five of the conversion schem[e]. A further move saw it go t[o] Fulwell depot at stage nine; i[t] remained in service there unt[il] stage fourteen. *Jack Gread[y]*

The K3s were synonymous wit[h] Edmonton depot. On the las[t] day of the 659 - 25th April 196[1] - K3 1695 turns from Pentonvill[e] Road into Caledonian Roa[d]; its journey started in Swinto[n] Street so this is why it is abou[t] to access Caledonian Road i[n] this manner. Normally 659[s] entered Caledonian Road fro[m] Grays Inn Road. Although th[e] remaining P1s were remove[d] from traffic at stage ten of th[e] conversion scheme the majorit[y] of the K3s were retained unt[il] stage eleven. *Jack Gread[y]*